Authenticity in Management:
Applications of the Psychology of Gestalt Therapy

Authenticity in Management

Applications of the Psychology of Gestalt Therapy

Brian O'Neill

Ravenwood Press

Developed and Published by the
Ravenwood Press a subsidiary of the
Illawarra Gestalt Centre.
Po Box 141 Peregian Beach
Queensland 4573
AUSTRALIA.

Cover illustration, text design and art work: B O'Neill

ISBN-13: 978-1484154908
ISBN-10: 1484154908
BISAC: Psychology / Industrial & Organizational Psychology

For more information on Ravenwood Press
Email: boneill@uow.edu.au
Website: www.illawarragestalt.org

 Or write to

Brian O'Neill
Illawarra Gestalt @peregian
Po Box 141 Peregian Beach
Queensland 4573
Australia

I   D e d i c a t i o n   I

This book is dedicated to Jim McKeown
who continues to inspire me
with his authentic wisdom and presence
as a manager.

I   Acknowledgement   I

I want to acknowledge all those who have shared with me
their insight, wisdom and compassion in being a manager,
those who have worked to manage me over the years -
and those who have allowed me the privilege to lead.

Authenticity in Management

Resource Articles

Authenticity in Management:
Applications of the Psychology of Gestalt Therapy

Introduction

This book offers my reflections, training and experience of over thirty years as both a manager and psychologist. I worked for many years as a manager in senior management roles in Government and Non-government organisations. I set up a network of Mental Health Community Rehabilitation services during the Richmond era of deinstitutionalisation in New South Wales, Australia; worked as a Health Service Director; was Head of the NSW State Drug Treatment Unit during the Drug Summit; Deputy State Director of Veterans Affairs counselling and more recently worked as a Senior Manager for Relationships Australia. As well as my management experiences I continued to work in my spare time as a psychologist and gestalt psychotherapy trainer. I have trained in Gestalt therapy and found this offers as much a way of life (like Buddhism) as a counselling approach. After many years experiencing these two fields as different I decided each informs the other. The bridge is living as a psychotherapist and manager "authentically".

My early understanding in the 1970s of being authentic was "being myself" - as the seventies quote went "you do your thing and I'll do mine". As I matured and reflected I realised this is one half of the equation. I am not "myself" alone. Authenticity in therapy, management and life is the dance with an "other" - in *suitable relationship*. Two of the world's most respected Gestalt therapy trainers, Erving and Miriam Polster, describe authenticity as *responsibly spontaneous* or *spontaneously responsive*. In essence we are ourselves alone and in relationships - be they couples, family, community, organisations and work. Theory guiding management practice presents management as a role. How management is defined appears non-authentic. At work you cannot just be yourself. As manager you have a special role to fulfil.. Yet delving deeper management and authenticity *in practice* is more a paradox than a role description. This is a "both/and" view rather than and "either/or". As we shall uncover, current management theories support authenticity in being a manager. Gestalt therapy offers principles and practices to guide the manager in being authentic and fits well with modern management theories of organisational culture, systems, contingency and complexity perspectives.

This book is my first endeavour to present theoretical and practical applications of Gestalt therapy in management. It offers managers to learn from the psychological methods of Gestalt therapy. I am sure psychologists and therapists who become managers may also benefit. I have developed chapters to explain Gestalt therapy (which can be complex) in simple terms. For those who are not knowledgeable about Gestalt therapy and wish to read further, I have included recent articles and book chapters in the second half of this book. They include a book chapter written with my colleague Dr. Seán Gaffney who works across the world as a Gestalt organisational consultant and has worked as a manager and therapist. Our book "*The Field Perspective: Methodology and Practice*" brings together our writing in therapy, groups and organisational consultancy. It is readily available through *CreateSpace* and Amazon.

I hope dear reader you find use and application of this book in your practice and if so I will be thankful

Brian O'Neill
Peregian Beach Queensland,
May 2013

The History of Management

Textbooks on management often describe management as arising with the Industrial Revolution in Europe. Before Industrialisation the Feudal and Agrarian societies existed and people had their place. Factory owners needed to "manage" people no longer governed by earlier feudal and tribal systems. However this is a Western view of history and minimises other cultures. In India and China there are older wisdoms of managing ourselves and others, no matter what position in society. These complex cultures had bureaucracies long before the Westminster system arose. They offer millennia of lived wisdom that applies equally today.

"In ruling people and serving Heaven,
nothing is like frugality.
Acting frugally is called 'Being ready early in the Morning.'

Tao Te Ching
Lao Tzu, page 101

"To arouse enthusiasm it is necessary for a man to adjust himself and his ordinances to the character of those he has to lead."

Book of Changes
Wilhelm, page 68

The history of management uncovers the cultural and social ground from which it develops, provides insight about what social meanings guide our ideas of management. Tracing the history of the words themselves provides the underlying beliefs and attitudes embedded in terms. Like the foundations of a house, the historical use of a word uncovers deeper collective social meaning of what it is to "manage" and "be managed".

The history of management documents two themes – *controlling others* and treating people with *indulgence and concern*. A third theme which arises later is management as a *skill and ability* running a business or organisation. As we shall see later in the book, this historical polarity between control and concern are central to the success of current management theories of complexity. They are equally central to a manager being authentic while still in the role of managing.

The Shorter Oxford Dictionary on Historical Principles (1973) is designed to trace the chronological sequence in developing meaning of words. This relates the significant stages of the meaning, place of origin and development of the word. It documents the source where a word was first used. This provides us with a unique perspective of the ground from which words develop and the accompanying phenomenology and social context.

The Shorter Oxford Dictionary on Historical Principles (1973) makes available the origin and use of the terms "manage" "management" "manager" and "managing". These show the original meaning and common use of these words and we might consider in what way these terms still hold meaning today and underpin our current theories and practice.

Manage: (1577) The training of a horse in its paces; (1579)To control the affairs of a household, institution etc; (1594) To cause persons or animals to submit to one's control; (1611) The skilful handling of a weapon; (1600) To conduct a war or an undertaking; (1649) To deal with carefully, to treat with indulgence or consideration; (1706) To bring over to one's wishes by artifice and flattery; (1899) To be so unskilful or unlucky as to do something, or contrive to get along or pull through under disadvantage.

Management: (1598) The action or manner of management; (1676) The use of contrivance for effecting some purpose, often in a bad sense, implying deceit or trickery; (1715) The power of managing, administrative skill, tact, ingenuity; (1818) Indulgence or consideration shown towards a person.

Manager: (1670) One skilled in managing affairs, money; (1705) One who manages a business or institution; (1793) A person appointed by a court to manage a business for the benefit of creditors.
Managing: (1715) addicted to scheming or to assuming the direction of affairs; (1754) Economical; (1768) Having executive control.

The term "mange" has the most detailed history of meaning. In the 16th century it means putting a horse through its paces and controlling a household or institution. These combined into meaning to cause a person or animal to submit to one's control. It is principally from a male perspective, pointing to this was the place of men to manage others - which exists in today's "glass ceiling" for women.

The dictionary recounts several instances where this word was used, for example when Bacon writes

"Young men in their conduct and manage of actions hold more than they can hold" (ibid, p. 1269).

In describing the control exerted by men over women, Tennyson writes

"Her father hadn't a head to manage" (ibid).

Disraeli provides the political bent in stating

"Managing mankind, by studying their tempers and humouring their weaknesses" (ibid).

Women were also managers (or more correctly a manageress) but specifically of theatres and brothels - no glass ceiling here.

Disraeli brings together two seemingly paradoxical uses of these terms. One theme is of controlling affairs, people and animals - sometimes neutral, at other times by trickery, and artifice. A second theme is to treat or deal with carefully, with indulgence and consideration. Disraeli combines these meanings by bringing *consideration and indulgence* with *control*. This becomes another form of *"artifice and ingenuity in controlling others to bring over to one's wishes"*.

Themes in the Meaning of "Management" over Time.
1. Control and submitting to control
2. Trickery, artifice and deceit
3. Deal with carefully and with indulgence or consideration
4. To bring over to one's wishes with artifice and flattery (combination of 2 and 3)
5. The power of managing, administrative skill, tact, ingenuity;

Many historians of management describe a pattern of theory development similar to that of Bowditch & Buono, (2011) where theories of management follow a time based developmental pattern. Earlier "classical" theories view human beings as economic units who are to be controlled and directed by their "betters" or managers. This view clearly came from the class system of 18th and 19th century Britain and the Industrial Revolution.

This in turn grew out a Feudal sense of ownership of people. People thinking they were free from a Feudal lord found themselves as "factory fodder" as they came to work in the cities. In many of the industrial cities of Britain and Ireland we can still see the small houses like human battery hen cages which housed workers in the 18th and 19th centuries.

Period	Pre-1800s	1800s	1800-1930	1930-1960	1970-2010	
Nature of Work	Agrarian	Industrial			Post Industrial	
Management theory	Pre-scientific	Classical		Neoclassical	Modern /Contemporary	
Specific Theories		Scientific management		Human relations	Management Science	
		Structuralist (Bureaucracy)		Behavioural	Total Quality Management	Systems Theory
		Administrative Theory		Quantitative management	Contingency Theory Organisational Culture	
Assumptions about human nature	Economic person	Social person		Self-actualizing person	Complex person	
Role of management	Control employee behaviour	Maintain employee social systems	Facilitate employee development	Ensure organisation integration	Facilitate organisational collaboration	

(Adapted from Bowditch, J.L. & Buono, A.F. (2011) "A Primer on Organisational Behaviour" 6th Edition, Wiley, New Jersey.)

In this developmental model the current era is modern managers - skilled and egalitarian - valuing staff and consumers alike. They are working to provide total quality and creatively adapting to the situation. They are the polar opposites found in earlier caricatures, such as Simon Legree of *Uncle Tom's Cabin.* Or the cruel mill owners of the North of England, brutally controlling workers for their own greed and advancement. Theorists see management progressing from older controlling forms to modern day humane approaches. This is presented in the following table:

Era	Classical	Neoclassic	Modern/Contemporary
Theories	Scientific management Structuralist (Bureaucracy) Administrative Theory	Human Relations Behavioural **Quantitative Management**	Management Science **Total Quality** Management Systems Theory Contingency Theory Organisational Behaviour and Culture
Historical meaning evident	Control and submitting to control Trickery, artifice and deceit	Deal with carefully and with indulgence or consideration	The power of managing, administrative skill, tact, ingenuity

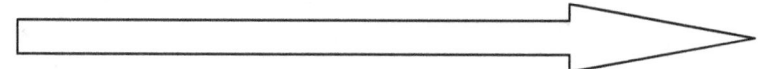

Movement forward in time

Contemporary approaches

The current literature has many definitions of management - some tailored to industry and commerce and others to the human services. A common definition is *management is both an art and science of achieving goals/getting things done through people*. This is a simple notion of management. Management like psychology has many theories about people and their nature. The philosophies underpinning definitions create the principles and practices of management. Thus philosophies of *control, productivity and surplus* create different management practices than those more humanistic. More current definitions have wider meaning than the earlier philosophies, for example:

> "PricewaterhouseCoopers defines a sustainable business enhances long-term shareholder value by addressing the needs of all its relevant stakeholders and adding economic, environmental and social value through its core business functions".
> *A revised philosophical perspective for management theory,*
> *Weymes, 2004 pp. 346-347*

Weymes defines a sustainable organisation as one which has:

- a clear purpose beyond profit;
- is driven by shared values; and
- is supported by systems and processes.

He states the proponents of sustainable organisations argue they need breakthrough thinking resulting in true innovation. This calls for partnerships, cooperation as well as open honest dialogue with stakeholders inside and outside the company. These organisations not driven by profit maximisation and will forgo short-term profit to ensure longer-term shareholder value. They are build trust with an aura of authenticity (his word) building a harmonious and family-like work environment. They are driven by a purpose, values and beliefs accepted by a wide range of societal interest groups and they encourage innovation. Gone are the days of bureaucracy and power based controls – replaced by modern managers who authentically act for the betterment of the staff.

Summary of Modern Theories (McMahon, 2011)

Modern or contemporary theories and approaches to management are described by McMahon as follows:

Quantitative Management emphasised mathematical approaches to managerial problem solving.

Organisational Behaviour focused on employee effectiveness through individual, group and organisational processes.

Systems Theory recognises the organisation as an open system dependant on the external environment for survival, and efficiency alone is not enough for survival. To be successful organisations have to be effective in ensuring a match between what they produce and what the external environment wants and needs.

Contingency Theory argues that best management practice depends on (or is contingent on) the situation. Technology employed by the organisation and the environment within which it works often influence the managerial action needed for success.

Total Quality Management emphasises the importance of improving quality to achieve competitive advantage. It could significantly reduce costs, focus on customer satisfaction and lead to huge quality gains - all of which benefit the organisation. For management, the focus is building total quality into every aspect of the organisation at every level. Quality becomes everyone's responsibility, not just those concerned solely with quality control.

Organisational Culture emphasises the role that an organisation's culture can play in shaping organisational success. It argues managers should shift their focus from structures and systems to concentrate on developing and sustaining cultural values that contribute to organisational success.

Most theories agree about the stages of development presented by Bowditch and Buono (2011).With this historical picture a directionality (past to present) and emphasis (control – maintain – facilitate) are obvious. To summarise one could say management theory (and practice) is moving from past to future in a developmental fashion. This is a shift from the controlling bureaucracy of the past to the self-actualising complex systems of the present - which are more humane and effective.

However there are alternatives views. The last 50 years of management adopting a more human approach appears true. Nonetheless management practice still uses controlling theories which emphasis performance and output. Organisations may attend to their social responsibilities within society, yet not at the expense of profit. Survival remains real for managers given the nature of human beings.

I have worked thirty years across community services, government and university sectors. Whatever management theory was espoused it became clear the management is less a movement forward and more like a house built block by block. The organisational structure is one of adding to "older" forms of historical management to not moving away from these.

The view the past has faded and new humane management processes are in operation is an illusion. This is similar to the visual illusion of an iceberg. With an iceberg we see what is above the surface - i.e. what current theories espouse - with the underlying implicit practices of bureaucracy control below the surface. Weymes argues the current financial crises and the resultant collapse of companies showed the underlying values and attitudes of greed and control of many financial organisations. Theoretically organisations promote the principles associated with total quality management and learning organisations. Yet the chief executive's primary focus fixates on control of the organisation to meet shareholder expectations.

Weymes believes management *theory* has become more "humane" with a focus on people and the importance of values, emotions and social responsibility. However at the bottom line organisations are unwilling to give up the controls associated with the bureaucratic organisation. So they work like the iceberg where above the surface is espoused modern humane management while at its heart lurks the classical theories of bureaucracy and control of employee behaviours. One might even wonder if further below the surface lies the Feudal and class systems accepted as the norm in countries such as Britain at the time of the Industrial Revolution.

Figure 1: The "Iceberg" of Management Theory in Practice

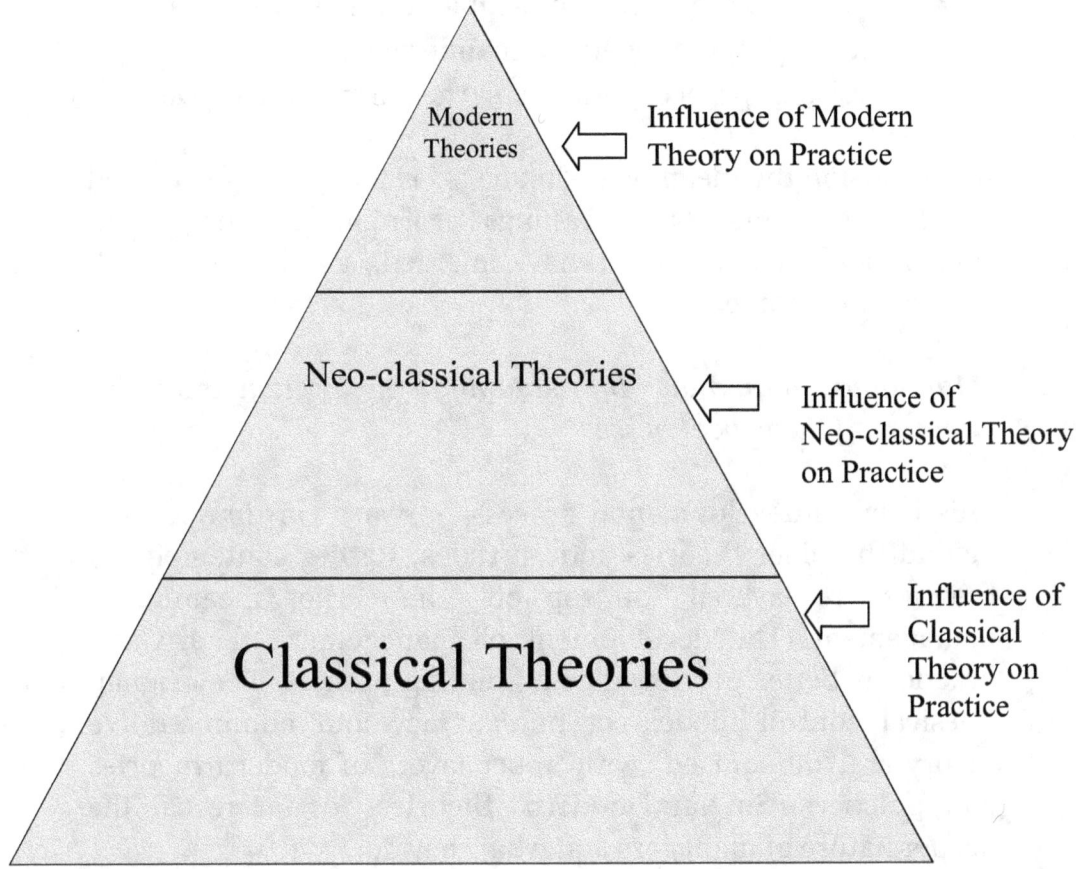

Petersen (2007) states the demands for control in modern management look similar to the descriptions used to diagnose autism –

- encompassing preoccupation with stereotyped restricted patterns of interest
- inflexible adherence to inflexible routines or rituals
- stereotyped and repetitive mannerisms
- persistent preoccupation with the parts of the object

In conclusion the meaning of "manage" is today a sophisticated yet polarised one. The meanings of "manage" being both *control* and *consideration* have merged, as they did with Disraeli, to become

"Managing mankind, by studying their tempers and humouring their weaknesses".

This is not a developmental process "forward" in time leaving behind the older theories and attitudes. Rather contemporary theories are layered "on top off" the earlier meaning of management. The development of management theory and practice is better portrayed as a building process. The original classical control models of bureaucracy and administrative theory are "humanised" with upper layers of modern theories and practices. So our "modern" theories do not reveal the deeper nature of managers and what they do.

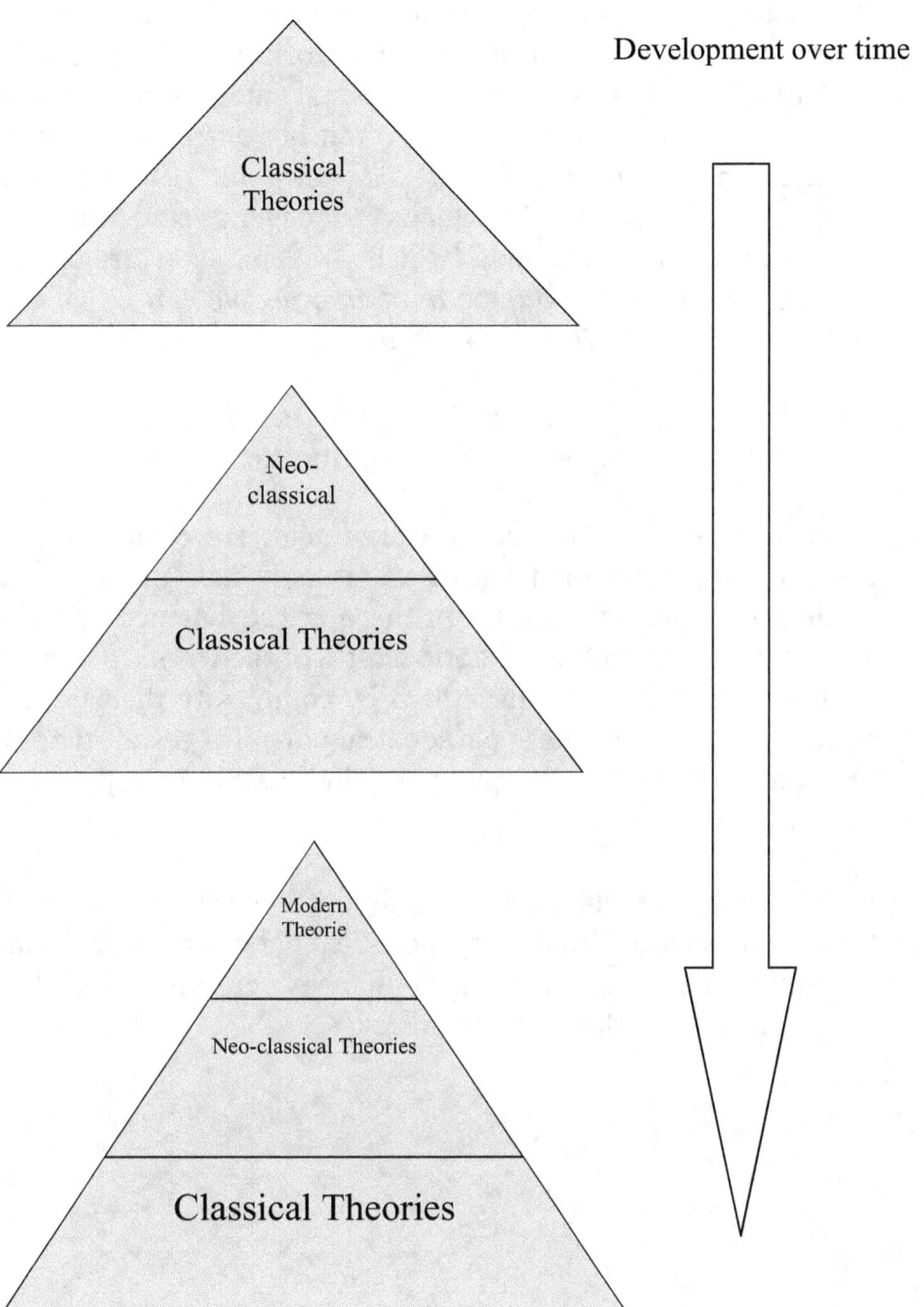

Development over time

To characterise management and managers in a fixed way in terms of either control or concern for workers is still primarily an "either/or" view. The reality of management and the world in general is we are in control *and* out of control. Complexity theories and Chaos theory offer a viewpoint of "both/and" rather than "either/or". Hence managers can be *both* controlling and concerned, (which are character traits and behaviours) and managers as *authentic people* can be all that and more. As Walt Whitman stated

> "Do I contradict myself? Very well, then I contradict
> myself, I am large, I contain multitudes."

Petersen offers a more complex argument. He considers how control itself is doomed because it is only half the story. In modern theories of complexity there is the balance between apparent control and the chaotic nature of the world to operate as a complexity. This is described by complexity theories and quantum physics. In these paradoxical polemics gestalt therapy provides theory and practice in psychotherapy *and* management.

In the following chapters we will outline the management theories in accord with the psychological perspectives of Gestalt therapy. We consider how they enhance each other, and their applications to working as a manager.

Gestalt Therapy and Management Theory
The Field and Systems Perspectives

Gestalt therapy might be expected to have developed theory on this subject because of its focus on organisational management. This is both through the Gestalt Institute of Cleveland (GIC) and the Gestalt International Study Centre (GISC) and the body of literature and training they have developed. The theory and practice of Gestalt OSD (*Organisation and Systems Dynamics*) or GIO (*Gestalt in Organisations*) is a field or application of Gestalt therapy which arose from a range of people around the world. Some of these are also gestalt therapists and some from a background of organisational consultancy. As Gaffney writes:

"The theory and practice of OSD is not necessarily a case of an individual therapeutic modality being used out of the context for which it was intended, and to which it should primarily be applied. It is, rather, a sibling if not a twin to gestalt therapy, one which can stand on its own feet, which always had developed and still is developing its own uniqueness. It was not and is not a distant cousin from an estranged branch of the family. Its core theoretical roots are the same. Its practice makes the same demands on its practitioners, though in the complex environments of groups, larger collectives and the individuals embedded in both of them"

The Gestalt Field Perspective: Methodology and Practice, Gaffney, 2013, p. 221.

As a Gestalt therapist and manager I have found around the world people who work in this area from a Gestalt perspective are organisational consultants. I am not an organisational consultant and I write as a therapist and a manager. My perspective is based on my work in management of counselling services within state and federal government and now within a large Non-government organisation.

I will also draw on work by Gestalt colleagues such as Seán Gaffney and their contributions in working as organisational consultants. I focus on the application of gestalt therapy to managing and being a manager. It is important to connect the rich literature and practice of Gestalt therapy to current management theory. There are several of management theories that connect with gestalt therapy -

- *Organisational Behaviour*

- *Systems Theory*

- *Contingency Theory*

- *Total Quality Management*

- *Organisational Culture*

In this chapter we consider *Organisational Behaviour* and *Systems* theories and applications to working as a manager. The theoretical lens of Gestalt therapy similar to these theories is the Field Perspective.

Organisational Behaviour and the Field Perspective

As defined by McMahon (2011) Organisational Behaviour theory focuses on employee effectiveness through individual, group and organisational processes. This management theory compares with counselling/psychology models and indeed much organisational psychology is precisely that. The importance of gestalt therapy theory in this area is in being one of the few therapies in which deals equally with individuals, dyads, groups, organisations and communities (O'Neill and Gaffney, 2013).

The Field Perspective in Gestalt Therapy

Psychology and counselling theory seeks to define the "self" of the person. Gestalt therapy's definition is *"the self is a system of contacts in the organism-environment field"*. Therefore when two or more people become systematised in their contact with each other, they are a "self" from this definition. For example a married couple is two individual selves and the relationship is like a third "self". To explain this in couples therapy training I use the metaphor of a rowing boat. The two people are in the relationship like being in a boat. If either moves they affect each other through being in the boat. When the third person, like a therapist, enters the boat they too move and are moved by one another. In couples counselling the "boat" of the relationship is invisible yet nonetheless affects those in it. This field perspective is in physics, where invisible forces of magnetism and gravity have a powerful impact on what appear disconnected objects such as planets.

This view of *self* allows the therapist (and manager) to see beyond the separate individual self of the person and see many "selves" which arise and come into being and then fade back into the ground. Biologically for example, a bee cannot survive long by itself and in reality it is more the bee hive which is the organism or *"self"* than individual bees.

31

As a gestalt therapist and manager I look at behaviour of the individuals in a workplace and the other "systems" or "selves". Managers can be aware of the individuals and the wider systems. In a workplace there are not only a collection of individual "selves" (like so many bees) but combined there is a bee hive or a "self" of the collective. This bee hive is as much a "self" as the individual, just more complex. As the "self" gets bigger, such as a State Government, there exists a wide field of bee hives.

Each of these "selves" in the organism/environment field has a culture that might be called a personality. So what, we might ask, is the personality of a team, a local council body, a Health Department? More importantly for a manager we can ask to what extent are issues in work practice primarily about the individual, or the work team or the organisation - or some interaction of all three. Back to biology, the behaviour of ants and bees makes more sense viewed in the light of the wider system of which they are part. While humans are no doubt more complex that ants and bees, it is the field perspective of gestalt therapy that allows the manager to see the wider patterns of the "self" of the team, work group or organisation. There is an interactive affect between the organisation, team and the individual worker on each other - and the manager themselves!

(You can read further in the essay entitled *"Drug Courts: A Commentary"* and the chapter on *"The Field Perspective"* in the Resource part of this book)

Systems Theory

Systems Theory recognised the organisation as an open system dependant on the external environment for survival, and emphasised that efficiency alone was not sufficient for survival. Similar to organisational behaviour theories and the field perspective, system theories seek to understand not only the individual behaviours but those of wider teams and systems, similar to our metaphor of the beehive.

Many traditional therapies since Freud have focused on the individual. They are usually viewed as a *patient* from a medical model world view. Rogers in the 1940's developed notions of the patient as a "client" and having some degree of capacity to influence and affect the therapeutic change themselves. Further developments with behaviour therapies focused on "healing" or therapy to individuals who are discrete separate units.

The development of "systems" theory as an alternative to the individual model has its roots in various influences which shaped its development. This includes a move away from a reductionist paradigm and a reaction against the iatrogenic impact of the medical model in therapy

Systems theory developed following the World War II from the work of Ludwig von Bertalanffy, Margaret Mead, Gregory Bateson and others. The impact of these approaches in working with couples and families led to family therapy, also referred to as couple and family therapy earlier referred to as marriage therapy. This branch of psychotherapy works with families and couples in intimate relationships to nurture change and development. It is interested in systems of interaction between family members. It emphasizes family relationships as an important factor in psychological health. Family problems have been seen to arise as an emergent property of systemic interactions, rather than to be blamed on individual members or an "illness".

Major models which have developed to form "schools" of family systems therapy are Minuchin's structural model, Whitaker's experiential model and Haley's strategic model. Other models integrated with these approaches, such as Narrative therapy, feminist theory, object relations theory, social constructivist theory, emotionally focused therapy & gestalt therapy amongst others.

The more common aspects of systemic thinking in psychotherapy are as follows (Lynch & Lynch, 2005) –

- A system is an interactional unit made up of individuals with a shared history, containing elements of power, intimacy, differentiation, and need satisfaction that are transmitted inter-generationally.
- The system is composed of various subsystems formed by such things as generational commonality (often) or gender, shared interests or compatibility.
- The primary subsystems in the family the couple system, the parental system and the sibling system. Other subsystems such as those formed by gender or mutual interests or needs, as secondary.
- Subsystems are regulated by boundaries, with intra and inter systemic rules (most often unstated).
- There is a natural hierarchy in the system. In general the adults are in the executive position in the system and the children are sub ordinates.
- Under stress, individuals and the system will repeatedly try to deal with a problem in old repetitive patterns, even if those methods have been only partially successful or failed in the past.
- Each subsystem has a unique function and purpose

Each of these systems has a function:

- The function of the marital system is provide emotional nurturance, and support between peers. Intimacy within this subsystem includes sex.

-The function of the parental system is to provide protection, nurturance, support, place, limits, permission, respect and love.

-The function of the sibling system is to learn to relate to peers, receive parental contacts and eventually differentiate and leave.
Dynamics of Intimate Relationships

The dynamics of intimate relationships helps in understanding of how couples form and the invisible forces that shape interactions. This is so in understanding the processes mediated by two theoretical constructs - the *attachment* which exists in the relationships (whether positive or negative) and the defined *boundaries* around people and sub-systems they are part of. These boundaries are the way a person or system defines who they are.

Systems of Relationships

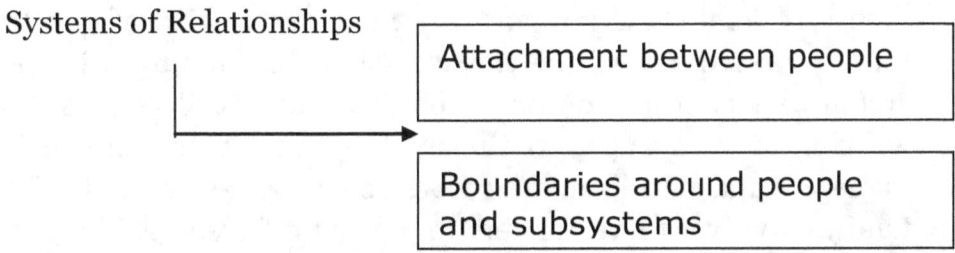

Attachment between people

Boundaries around people and subsystems

The dynamics of the system are reflected in the sequences and patterns of interaction. They are not cause and effect but more like stimulus response, happening in chains of behaviour and reaction.

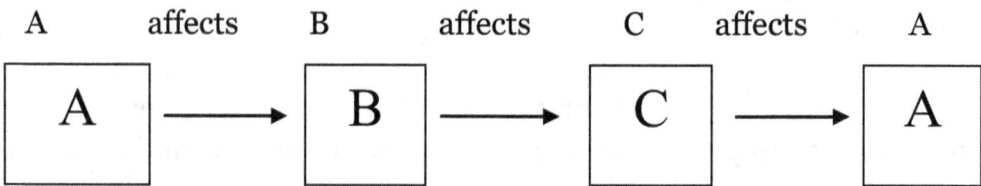

A   affects   B   affects   C   affects   A

A → B → C → A

Behaviour is understandable in interaction given the context and the sequence or chain of interactions. Behaviour neither is nor pathologised, as with the medical model. When viewed through the lens of attachment between people in the system, then the behaviour, which may seem paradoxical, makes sense. For example people will stay in what looks like unpleasant relationships because the underlying attachment bonds exist holding them together.

The Gestalt Therapy Field Perspective and Management.

There are subtle yet important differences between the system theory of family therapy and the field perspective of gestalt therapy, and these will be explained later. Beginning with the system theory basics outlines above, let us translate these to working as a manager in the work setting. Some theorists, managers and staff liken their work colleagues as being "like" a family. However there are very important differences. The first of these is the underpinning force which guides paradoxical behaviours noted in family therapy due to *attachment*. Attachment bonds between families are of course much more complex and enduring than those in a workplace. Confusion arises when staff or managers act "as if" they are the same which is unfortunate.

In one case I was being interviewed for a position as a director of operations. The CEO commented our relationship would be similar to that of a husband and wife - this set off immediate alarms bells on my part. As a Couples therapist I know the challenges such a relationship brings. Also the power differential between two married partners and a boss and subordinate are significantly different.

Therefore while the team is not a family, the principles of systems theory translate to assessing and intervening with patterns of complex systems in a workplace in the same way. Consider the common elements of systems theory outlined by Lynch above and how they may be applied to the work setting. This includes the heightened awareness they offer a manager. These common principles, adapting to the differences between work relationships and family relationships, offer assessment of patterns which managers may consider intervening with. This is possible once they understand the underlying dynamics of how the workplace systems are operating. The principles below have been changed from a family to suit a workplace.

- A system is an interactional unit made up of individuals with a shared history, containing elements of power, intimacy, differentiation, and need satisfaction that are transmitted inter-generationally.

Two of the most important patterns of how a system works are *Homeostasis* and *Growth*. A third pattern in humans systems is those that are Ego-centred and usually manifest in the need for power and control.

This clearly is not exclusive to families but also groups and many other situations of collections of people - most certainly organisations and the workplace. When I join an organisation - and even before when I research the position I am applying for and people who work there - I begin to see patterns that are important to me as a possible manager.

For example I am interested to see clues to the cohesion in managing the organisation - have the last two or three CEO's left in short periods of time or the Board frequent turnover. This tells me the organisation is in rough waters and needs a sense of stability. It leads me to question the factors causing this. Most times it will be issues of power and control and personality. I look at the financial situation across the last annual reports as a sign of the functioning and stressors within this wider field.

As I join a new workplace I am open to hear the history of past workers and managers and their relationships to other organisations. How are they perceived - is there is a collusive, confluent "us against the world" language or are people able to differentiate seeing themselves and others as *different yet the same*. Can they allow for and accept differences both inside and outside the organisation. This applies when contacting the organisation's partners and representatives, particularly those whom we will work closely with and may be important to our continuing existence - such as funding providers or key clients.

These perspectives may be indicative of the current present situation and reflect an ongoing attitude – showing patterns of behaviour which is historically based yet no longer valid. One regional office in the organisation in which I worked had a history with managers who quickly came and left. Staff developed an attitude and behaviour towards managers which was *"you'll not stay like the rest of them - you'll leave us - why should we make the effort"*

In such circumstances the manager, workers and staff must attend to this rather than let it go underground and work in a hidden ways They can instead consciously work with such attitudes and most importantly start with accepting that they make sense. As we will see later, any attempt to challenge the logic underlying emotional dynamics of a system which is informing people's behaviours is counter-productive. Such is the strength of forces such as attachment bonds that they need to be acknowledged not fought against. The new manager may indeed leave – particularly if they shame people for their feelings of loss and abandonment. We will expand on this further is considering topics such as Working Alliance as well as shame based fields.

In such circumstances hearing and accepting the history and behaviour allows a balancing process to influence the field. There may be wisdom in apparent "negative" attitudes and behaviours.

- The system is composed of various subsystems formed by such things as generational commonality (often) or gender, shared interests or compatibility.

This is a useful for a manager to be aware of in organisation they are joining. While certain subgroups are understandable and formed by people's position description or official roles within the workplace, there are many invisible subgroups which form. Some arise from the history of the organisation (i.e. "we used to work together"); some from outside the workplace (i.e.

"we play for the same team)' some from common beliefs or attitudes (i.e. "we need to stick together as we are women/unionists/gay or lesbian/catholic etc).

These subgroups also can create the "glass ceiling" of an organisation. I have seen this with gender (less or even *more* women); religion (at a certain level only people from the Church get high level positions); political affiliation (once the election happens the top level people will change); or other relevant subgroups. These subgroups can also be the "coffee brigade" where Robyn Hood and her Merry Men gather in the "glen" of the coffee shop and say what they *really* think about the Manager (Prince John) - as they long for the return of a previous manager - King Richard.

- The primary subsystems in the workplace are the hierarchy of executive system, the management system and the staff system. Other subsystems such as those formed by gender or mutual interests or needs, as secondary as described previously

These *organisational systems* are defined by the position descriptions and organisational structure of management and staffing. The organisation defines who belongs in each system, the rules and roles governing each subsystem and the way each system interacts with the other. In some systems I have worked in such as Health Services, the relationships between levels are marked and in the National Capital people even mix after work according to their "rank" within the system and define themselves by whichever level they are. In one Federal Government management position I was cautioned by the director to not mix with staff at lunch time in the lunchroom. I was an EL 1 (executive level 1) and they were APS levels

(Australian Public Service) and were "below me". This is reminiscent of the class and Feudal system of Britain. Lords and Ladies were above the professional class and working class and each stayed within their own class.

At the other polarity some organisations may be able to reduce the hierarchy, at least within certain ranks of staffing. At the university I worked at for example it was a seemingly open workplace. Academics, and tutors, lecturers, senior lecturers, associate professors, professors, deans were all open relating with each other on a *relatively* equal basis. We also socialized, unlike the other organisations mentioned. However it became clear after a while that this relative egalitarian society did not extend to administration and general staff such as gardeners and security guards. They were not part of this "equal" system. As the famous line from George Orwell's *Animal Farm* goes - "some animals are more equal than others."

From my experiences over thirty years management theory has become more "humane" focusing on the importance of values, emotions and social responsibility. Yet at the bottom line organisations are unwilling to give up the controls associated with the bureaucratic organisation. So they work like the iceberg where above the surface is espoused modern humane management while at its heart lurks the classical theories of bureaucracy and control of employee behaviours. Perhaps the submerged power and status are a reflection of an older, deeper social norm of Feudalism. The Industrial Revolution "freed" people as serfs and servants opening the wider class system of professional workers. Today's society appears more equal yet within organisations the Bureaucratic model of management mirrors older systems of class and Feudalism. This is understandable as these historical forms of being "managed" existed for millennia and may be deep within the human psyche.

- Subsystems are regulated by boundaries, with *intra* and *inter* systemic rules (most often unstated).

This language sounds technical yet the simple reality is any subsystems which develop often does so organically without conscious intent or definition. This may be the people who sit together at lunch or go out for coffee which forms a solid bounded group after a time. These are organically formed and are not necessarily negative as with Robyn Hood. In fact these subgroups can form a part of the fabric of staff feeling supported in the workplace. How to be a part of these groups is not always clear and these subgroups can also become negative when they are the source of complains and gossip which are not brought to wider teams and managers/coordinators. Some small subgroups can also wield significant power and influence in a workplace, when the members have a high or even feared standing within the wider team or organisation. This is also so when organisational bullying arises not just from a single person but from a subgroup and this can be a passive process of ostracising people as well as actively bullying.

Recently a CEO wrote a commendation on the web site of an executive coach. She stated she had felt bullied and ostracised by her group of managers who reported to her and was in a dark space until she worked with the coach. While writing this on a web page may show a lack of judgement, it does present a picture of how such subsystems can work again a manager. Even when they hold more presumed power through their position - there can be as much power in a lower status as a higher one.

One of the first patterns I look for in joining an organisation is does someone I am managing want my job and didn't get it. If this is handled properly the person can be succession planned and become an ally. However if this remains hidden or goes to the sympathetic subgroup of the person then it will make my job difficult until it can be dealt with. This may have been the cause of the lack of support and "dark space" the CEO experienced. As another CEO friend once said to me "well if they want my job, try doing their own one first!"

The opposite is a well functioning subgroup, particularly a leadership team of the organisation. This, from my experience, is a joy to behold for any senior manager. Such a team is worth gold. I have come up with some metaphors that define this which I find helpful.

A metaphor for teamwork is people in a boat rowing together. You might be lucky enough to be Ulysses or Boadicea and the people row not just to serve the king or queen but because they know the king or queen have the vision that will hold them all. They row the boat and will follow their leader as they know they serve a higher purpose. When the boat sinks everyone wants to save the king or queen.

Or the team might be like a Roman Slave Galley with Caesar or Cleopatra, where the rowers are slaves and there is a large man with a whip making sure everyone obeys. If the ship sinks people look after themselves and may even hope the ruler drowns.

If you are the captain of the Titanic in a lifeboat with a gun and people are scrabbling into the boat to survive, the sailors may probably support you but at the end people are looking to survival, - not the best interests of the captain or the boat and may swamp it and it sinks.

The metaphors go on and you might create your own - from the HMAS Pinafore in Gilbert and Sullivan to elite rowing athletes in the Olympics - what boat are you managing currently?

- There is a natural hierarchy in the system. In general the adults are in the executive position in the system and the children are subordinates.

As with families there are hierarchies in all organisations. Even when the hierarchy is flat there are those who stand out as leaders. An organisation's mandated hierarchy is not however a "natural" hierarchy - it is imposed by the organisation. Thus the manager must also establish themselves as being both appointed and "natural" to be in their role. This is like the new, "wet behind the ears" lieutenant and the battle hardened sergeant we see in movies - unless the sergeant and lieutenant come to an understanding there is hell to pay when they go to war. A "smart" new lieutenant will know to attend to and learn from the sergeant and be mentored.

- Under stress, individuals and the system will repeatedly try to deal with a problem in old repetitive patterns, even if those methods have been only partially successful or failed in the past.

From a gestalt therapist perspective there are many reasons for this and this will be discussed further. This is the case when developing a working alliance with peoples/systems when faced with change. The work of the manager is to to not only manage but lead, even if seemingly from behind. People will cling to processes in organisations for a sense of survival and security - we first need to see this and acknowledge this - it has had its uses. With gestalt therapy, a key to change is to sacrifice security for a readiness for change and a willingness to experiment. When all else fails it is hard to say no to "lets try it for six months and if it doesn't work we will go back to the old system." In gestalt therapy there is a change model termed paradoxical change. This considers change can happen as we let go of older ways of functioning and allow new ones to emerge.

I was in a service where students now did the intake of clients - much to the displeasure of the admin staff who had previously done this. It was annoying as the students were acting as "volunteers" and could choose not to turn up - which left the admin staff to do it anyway. We held a team meeting to discuss it just before the Christmas break - it was fully attended as it was a hot issue sorely contended. Every single person had a chance to speak. There was acknowledgement of both sides and people agreed to continue with the students doing it. Yet after the break when people returned from holidays, miraculously the admin staff began doing the intake and everyone else accepted this. In gestalt therapy terms this is called *paradoxical change* - change happens when we accept what is, rather than trying to be what we are not. The group that pushed the students to do intake had somehow heard the admin and while they were bigger in numbers had nonetheless changes organically.

- Each subsystem has a unique function and purpose

This simple principle brings us to an understanding of the key shift from a systems perspective to a field perspective. So far the systems language of subsystems discusses subsystems as groupings of individuals - like ping-pong balls bumping against one another or little bags of ping-pong balls (teams) bumping against one another.

The subtle shift from systems to a field perspective is the definitions are less separate, concrete boundaries (like balls) and more fluid like water or energy fields. So a field perspective views people are *both* physically separate (and thus subgroups are like a collection of these separate parts) - and at some level are connected, merged and a part of one another. Field theory describes people and subsystems like droplets of water falling as rain, which then preserve their essence as they combine into an *oneness* when they form a river or ocean.

We will describe this further later in the book.

Gestalt Therapy and Management Theory
Total Quality Management and Organisational Culture

> *"Total Quality Management* emphasises focus on customer satisfaction and lead to huge quality gains, all of which benefit the organisation. In terms of management, the focus is on building total quality into every aspect of the organisation and at every level so that quality becomes everyone's responsibility, not just the responsibility of those concerned solely with quality control."

> *"Organisational Culture* emphasises the role that an organisation's culture can play in shaping organisational success. It is argued that managers should shift their focus from structures and systems and concentrate their efforts on developing and sustaining cultural values that contribute to organisational success."

I remember my early days in management in the NSW Health Service and the introduction of the Total Quality Management approach. I was joining organisational committees addressing quality assurance with the buzzword being "quality". Looking back, this "new" approach assumed that people were not focused on quality and now would be. The defining difference was the attention to customer, consumer or client satisfaction. This included collecting client satisfaction surveys and being willing to hear from the client and consumer their evaluation of our service. This developed an emphasis on consumer or client involvement - in strategic planning and business or service development – and the impact is till with us today in management in one form or another.

Early client evaluations of quality were simplistic and did not inform managers about changes in the organisation or service. It became clear later the "*what*" of satisfaction being measured was important. This is now reflected in the Kirkpatrick levels which note important distinctions in measurement of quality and results. Evaluation is considered four different levels (the "Kirkpatrick levels") listed below. Note the further down the list, the more valid the evaluation.

- Reaction - What does the person feel about the service?

- Learning - What facts, knowledge did the person gain?

- Behaviors - What skills did the person develop, that is, what new information is the person using?

- Results or effectiveness - What results occurred, that is, did the person apply the new skills to the necessary tasks what results were achieved.

I later realised these evaluations were also applicable in evaluating the "quality" of therapy and mental health interventions. I found this specifically in the literature and research of the Working Alliance and outcomes. The research found the best indicator of positive outcome was the client's rating of the working alliance with the service provider. This connects the principles of Total Quality Management with the importance of what achieves results for the customer or service user. Thus the staff must in essence adapt to and be informed as the best indicator of good outcome (quality) - the client.

Total Quality Management and Working Alliance.

Inderbitzen (1990) notes Hippocrates, Galen and Plato all emphasised the relationship between the physician and the person as being in itself a therapeutic factor that underlies the effectiveness of all the physicians other skills. Freud (1940) developed the idea of a therapeutic alliance. He noticed in working with people experiencing schizophrenia that even amid such chaotic disorder there exists in some corner of the mind a functional aspect of the person. He states the therapeutic TASK is to emphatically seek out the non psychotic part of the ego, establish a meaningful communication and nurture its growth and expansion.

This explanation by Freund offers a step-by-step set of guiding principles working with ANY disordered system, be they individual, couple, family, group, team, work group, organisation or community. In systems language we could say -

- emphatically seek out the functional part of the system,
- establish a meaningful communication and relationship
- and nurture its growth and expansion.

Principles of developing Working Alliance

The literature on therapeutic alliance has in the last several decades included work with suicide, major depression, personality disorder, affective disorder and schizophrenia. Several studies link therapeutic alliance with positive outcome in treating serious mental illness, in particular schizophrenia. Authors have defined a *relationship* element of alliance (as described by the psychoanalytic and client-centred therapy schools), and a *task* element (as found in behaviour therapy literature). Others define therapeutic alliance as comprising both task and relationship. Therefore alliance is the bond between therapist and client (*relationship*) and the agreement between them on the goals and tasks of the therapeutic endeavour (*task*).

In a meta-analysis of 24 studies, Horvath and Symonds found a correlation between therapeutic alliance and outcome across all types of measure of outcome. This was not a function of the type of therapy practiced. The measure which was most predictive of treatment outcome was based on the clients' assessments of alliance, while ratings by therapists were less predictive and ratings done by observers least predictive of outcome.

Other studies show little correlation between staff and client perceptions of alliance, with the client perception as the critical factor in predicting outcome. The most commonly used assessment tool for the working alliance is the Working Alliance Inventory (WAI) by Hovarth and Greenberg. The key elements in this assessment which are the principle defining constructs are –

- Relationship
- Goal
- Task
- Problem Definition

Working Alliance Grid

These four key principles used to define a working alliance can be viewed pictorially in a grid. This working alliance grid can guide the therapist and be used in supervision (O'Neill, 1992).

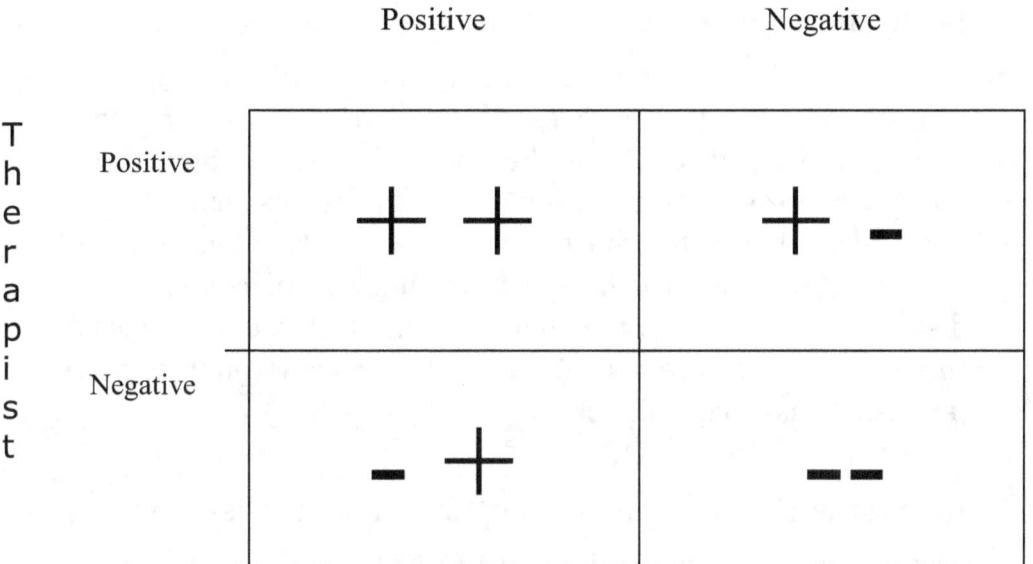

Client/Family/System/Organisation

The four quadrants define different spaces within the Working Alliance field.

In Quadrant 1 the symbols ✛ ✛ indicates both the therapist and the client/system are in an agreed alliance around the four dimensions of relationship, goal, task and problem definition.

In Quadrant 2 the symbols. ✛ ▬ indicates the therapist has a sense of alliance but not the client. In this case the therapist has developed a plan, worked out tactics in supervision and is relatively sure they have the inside track on what the issues are for the client/system. The more this happens and the more this is out of sync with the client/system, the more the therapeutic alliance will deteriorate and in this case the client will terminate, both during the session by disengaging and then by not attending, missing appointments and not attending.

In Quadrant 3 the symbols **-** **+** indicates the client has a sense of alliance with the therapist but the therapist is dissatisfied. In these cases the cause of the therapist misalignment is through the therapist's dissatisfaction with the therapy process. Previously (Quadrant 2) the misalignment has been through the therapist's satisfaction with their sense of therapy direction, which was unfortunately disconnected or disjoined in relation to the client/system. In the early stages of this work this is rarely a relational disconnection and is more problem/task/goal disjunction.

In Quadrant 4 the symbols **-** **-** show both parties are not in accord. In these cases this is either because the situations in Quadrants 2 and 3 have gone unattended and the relationship has deteriorated into quadrant 4 OR the situational aspects of the therapy setting are set up to create this in some form. This is obvious in situations of mandated clients in a system which does not see a need for alliance or has very fixed limits around intervention – if you don't do it OUR way then there is no alternative.

Application to Management

I have found Working Alliance is an equally powerful principle and practice in the management sphere. In working with systems and subsystems as described in the previous chapter the Working Alliance is applied to staff and subsystems. The Working Alliance can thus apply in how as a manager we work with an individual who is struggling with whom we must engage in performance management. Equally this is a subgroup or team who are struggling with a manager or with other individuals, subgroups or teams. This also applies in working effectively with other organisations and developing strategic alliances.

This principle and practice of a working alliance underpins contract management and this is what is referred to as B.A.T.N.A. - *Best Alternative To Negotiated Agreement.* The skills needed to achieve this require working with the polarities which the person, system or organisation displays. When a person or system is struggling it is because they are caught between wanting to do something and not wanting to do it. This is a widespread process underlying much resistance to change. It tells managers of the paradoxical behaviours people display when they seem convinced of feeling, thinking and behaving one-way yet end behaving in another.

When we can learn to accept and even expect people will be multivalent in their motivation we can then enquire or look for the polarity which may not be obvious. With this view people are less likely to let us down and we are more likely to be accepting that they are pro **and** con, positive **and** negative, for **and** against. Once we can remove ourselves from the person or group's struggle we can explore with the person, group of team both choices, both polarities.

This ability to see both aspects of an issue for a person or team supports a motivational interviewing approach to issues. In this approach the pros and cons of changing and not changing are explored. As a manager if we are committed fully to ONLY one-way we will (and do) meet with resistance. Being flexible with ourselves and others allows opportunity to change, adapt and thus increase the quality.

Culture, Community and the Field Perspective

In an organization the **parts** (people and subgroups) are placed in positions of power. They are called on to exercise power in deciding for the **whole**. These decisions, even when "voted" for or reached by consensus, are nonetheless decisions of conscious intent of the **parts**. They may not be in touch with the more elusive, implicit functioning of the **whole**. This is perhaps the prime difference between an organization and a community – an organization is organized by mainly explicit forces, while a community, in a sense "happens". At times the organization functions implicitly as a community and at other times more explicitly as an organization, with Board meetings, politics, agendas and business meetings.

From experiences in areas of management, organisational culture and community involvement, I sense the difference when the endeavor of a collective seems mainly that of being a community or an organization. Each of these, both the organisation and the community, can be said to have a "culture" yet there are important differences between the culture of a community and that of an organisation. This discrimination is important, if the collective believes they are functioning as one (that is a community) when they are the other (an organization). This discrimination is also functionally important in being aware of the contact between these processes of *organizing* and *being in community*.

The difference between an individual and a collective carries distinct challenges. In working with organisations from a Gestalt perspective there are important differences compared to individual therapy. For example Maurer (2008) notes that while the fundamental human need of relationship with others is present in organisations, it exists in counterpoint to an important need for survival. As he points out –

> *With some notable exceptions, organizations do a poor job of living up to the values they set for themselves, even when they are sincere in creating these statements. One reason they don't live up to their value statements is the statements themselves: they fail to take the whole picture into account.*

> *(Maurer, 2008, page 44).*

From Maurer's perspective this "whole picture" involves an essential polarity of our nature, striving for relationship and the greater good, while looking out for self interest. This survival need will at times overshadow the best interests of others. As he states, the value statements of organizations which enshrine trust, respect and understanding need to be held alongside other self-interested behaviours, which include positioning, cunning and deceit.

Positioning, Cunning and Deceit.

Working with the various people and subsystems leads us to hope for the best in people's relationships and thus developing a positive culture. At the same time the person, for various reasons may be motivated to a reflex of survival and behave in ways that are indeed deceitful, cunning or about achieving power and position. If we extend this view to see the individual and the wider organisation in which they exist then the person's behaviours may be a reflection of the wider field they finds themselves. If the organisation allows for survival reactions from people and doesn't push against these, the person may reduce their need for cunning and deceit.

One of the founders of Gestalt psychology, Wertheimer, states a profound and simple fundamental principle of the gestalt approach -

> *"There are wholes, the behavior of which is not determined by that of their individual elements, but where the part – processes are themselves determined by the intrinsic nature of the whole"*
>
> *(Wertheimer, 1925 in Ellis 1938, p. 2)*

If we translate this to a workplace we can say -

> There are wholes (the service or organisation) the behavior of which is not determined by that of their individual elements (the people or staff) but where the part – processes (individuals, subsystems etc) are themselves determined by the intrinsic nature of the whole (the organisation)

This sets a context remembering about management theory and practice becoming more "humane" with a focus on people yet unwilling to give up the controls associated with the bureaucratic organisation. If management espouse modern humane management while at its heart lurks the classical theories of bureaucracy and control of employee behaviours then this will affect the field of the organisation. An organisations espousing staff-centred approaches yet nonetheless reverting to being controlling is in essence being deceitful – even if for its survival. So not only people but organisations can be cunning, deceitful and positioning.

Survival versus relationship is not solely about staff behaving this way but also the organisation of which they are apart. The antidote is not to try to dismiss or get rid of the survival of individuals and the organisation of which they are a part. As Maurer suggests it is to allow for both, make space for both and allow both. This paradoxical acceptance of such polarities in individuals and organisations requires a degree of relinquishing *some* control, and as we shall see in the next chapter, where managers are being in control by allowing for not being in control at the same time - paradoxical intention.

Gestalt Therapy and Management Theory
Contingency Theory

> *"Contingency Theory* argues that best management practice depends on or is contingent upon the situation at hand."

Traditional Contingency Theory of management promotes the ability of the manager to choose different management approaches to suit the situation. When I was training in management in the 1980s this took the form of a chart wherein managers would choose to move from being directive, consultative or laissez-faire depending on what type of management issue arose.

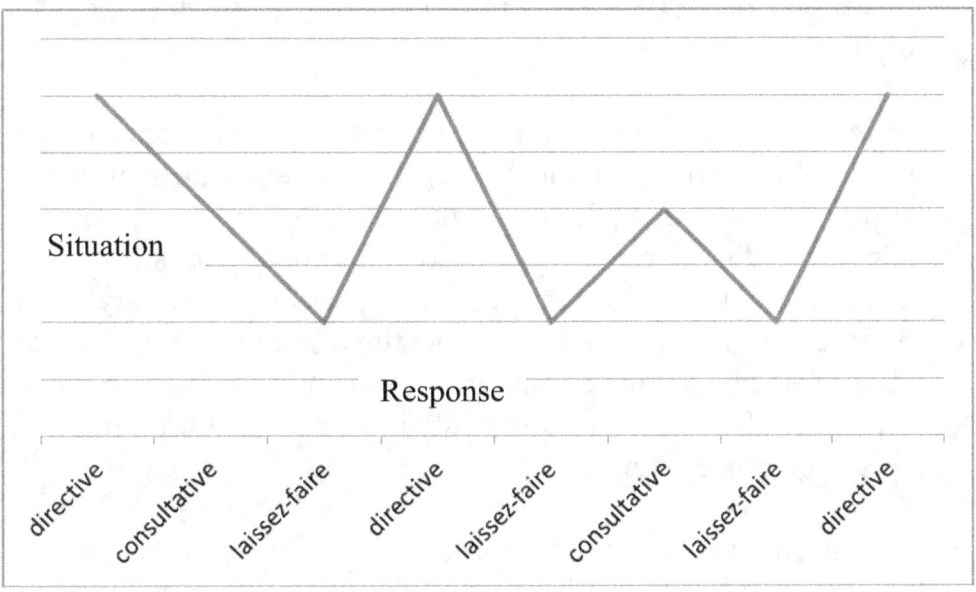

This made sense at the time yet on reflection there are several flaws or at best questions about this approach to management. First how to know which approach suits which situation? In some cases such as strategic planning it seems obvious that one would take a consultative approach, when we need to access the greater wisdom of the team we would hopefully be laissez-faire and in situations which needed leadership and vision we would step for in a more directive mode.

However in my experience most people, as with therapy, have a certain style or reflex that suits their personality and background experience. Further if we try to be eclectic and learn various approaches we may become a jack of all trades. What do we do as a manager if we decide to be laissez-faire but staff criticise us for not showing leadership? What at first seems a simple adaptable approach may in the end lead us to be a lukewarm manager who in the end does not fit the organisation.

From a field perspective, some organisations work from specific organisational models almost as a given. An extreme example is being laissez-faire in the army may not be well received and being too directive in collaborative organisation such as a university will not suit. Yet no matter what style of management organisations espouse the argument remains that underneath all organisations are the need for people to be in charge and follow more classical behavioural and bureaucratic models of management.

An alternative argument found in modern management theories used Chaos theory to challenge the idea of an organisation or a leader/manager being in control. This management perspective also fits with the principles and theory of gestalt therapy. Let us pursue and develop this further. I have found these more sophisticated models of Chaos and Complexity theories of management move away from the "either/or" of control/not control to a "both/and" view. This is more contingency theory based than the reductionist idea of the wise manager "choosing" the approach to use with steadiness and grace.

Petersen (2007) considers much of the *control* approach in classical and neo-classic theory is doomed. He argues it is only half or part of the story. Modern theories of complexity need balancing between our seeming control and the nature of the world to work as a complexity - recently described by Chaos theories and quantum physics. It is with these two paradoxical polemics that gestalt therapy has a history of theory and practice both in psychotherapy and organisational consultancy. Further this not a necessarily modern approach as the Taoist writings present a mature cultural sensitivity to the "management" of people many hundreds of years ago which is dictated by this polarity of "control/not control".

> *"There are those who want to control the world by action.*
> *But I see they cannot succeed.*
> *The world is a sacred vessel*
> *It should be not interfered with*
> *To interfere is to spoilt it*
> *To grasp it is to lose it."*
>
> Tao Te Ching
> Lao Tzu

Contingency Management and Gestalt Field Perspective

These theories about control/not control are well expressed by Gaffney (2013) when he writes of the different forms of change in an organisation -

> *"Traumatic* change occurs when unexpected and uncontrollable events set in motion a chain reaction with a life of its own. For a period of time, the organization is only capable of responding to external stimuli and all sense of agency may – at least temporarily – disappear. The locus of control is clearly not within the organization or its leadership. External driving forces appear to have the upper hand. The situation goes from bad to worse, then worse again. The organization may implode, as Enron did. Or explode, like Lehmann Brothers, firing dangerous shrapnel in all directions. Sooner or later, the drama of traumatic change will segue into either organic or planned change.
>
> *Organic* change is that which occurs naturally, is always occurring and may not even be noticed except retrospectively. People change over time. Staff turnover settles into a rhythm that seems normal. Market trends come and go. Depending on whether your paradigm for people in organizations is theory X or Y (or whatever letter of the alphabet is in vogue), management will trust organic change always to work for the best of the organization and its members – or will predict chaos, sabotage, laziness and disaster.
>
> *Planned* change is much loved by top management. Planned change is always imposed by the few onto the

many, usually cascading down from the very top onto senior executives, then onto the next level downwards in the hierarchy. At some stage, middle management will feel the blast of air as the cascade approaches and then they in turn direct it downwards. It is always presented as "good" for the organization and maybe even for the many, those whom it affects the most. It can often be "necessary", even "essential to our survival". Planned change is usually accompanied by schedules, benchmarks, deadlines, measurable progress charts and reports.

Emergent change is the name I am giving to a hybrid of *Organic* change and comparatively trauma-free *Planned* change. This is where the extent, range, direction and details of possible and also desired change emerge from within the organization itself and thus inform the planning of support for these changes to occur. "

(Gaffney, 2013, pgs. 390-391)

Gaffney's work as an organisational consultant if firmly rooted in Gestalt therapy and the field perspective. To develop this further, let us thus review this from a gestalt therapy perspective and translate into the management arena.

The Quest for Control

The idea that our world is predictable and that we are in control of it is a fundamental premise for science and Western culture and is supported by the extent to which more and more is achieved by science and technology. Yet similar Maurer critiques of organisations not taking survival needs into account, Gaffney critiques the premise that a manager and organisation can be "in control" of the organisation and run it. This premise of being in control underpins many if not all the Classical and Neo-classic theories of management; no matter how much they aspire to be different. Petersen (2007) argues that modern management theory has become like a house of mirrors in a carnival which shows distorted pictures of reality and so the validity of such theories are low. One of the criticisms he levies is that, similar to Maurer in the USA, writers in Britain have found public service organisations to be more attentive to self-interest. He cites Le Grand (2003) who in one study found those working in the public sector saw people no longer as altruistic but as acting from self-interest. Service users were seen as demanding "customers" with rights and complaints rather than people with needs. This change goes hand and hand with approaches that manage public services as market based entities.

He critiques how the "quest for control" of scientific rationality has lead to the belief to find cybernetic control over social processes, making it possible to gain control of the future of society (and organisations) using intelligent planning and sophisticated tools. He gives as examples approaches such as business process re-engineering; total quality management; balanced score cards; performance management; lean management; and knowledge management schemes. This quest for control displays as:

- Explicit goals and details tasks
- Complete description of all activities
- Achievement of tangible results
- Measurement and evaluation
- Correction to achieve results

Petersen argues the acceptance of such philosophies and practices show a disturbing view of what management is about – controlling people and systems. Second, and perhaps more importantly, the result for managers is they will follow policy and procedures based on control, no matter how humane looking. Finally my own criticism of this which I have witnessed is the lack of *reflection* by managers and organisations of the principles and philosophies that are guiding what they do. Rather than look deeper to the underlying philosophical assumptions on which so much management theory and practice are based, most managers and organisations are determined to "manage". Our earlier definitions were:

"Management is both an art and science of achieving goals/getting things done through people"

It is the focus on "getting things done" that holds the embedded implication that managers can and do use art and science to achieve results and get things done.
As Gaffney writes:

> "The difficulty I have with planned change, both as a manager and as an OD consultant, is twofold:
>
> First, it is being imposed can often lead to a traumatic impact with all of its drama, paralysis, and disempowerment. Second, planned change in its planning and scheduling ignores the basic reality *that organic change is anyway always occurring*. The fact of introducing news of a planned change is already changing the conditions which are supposedly to be changed, though the wishful thinking is that this is in a

particular, planned and predictable way. Despite previous experience of unpredictable or unwanted responses to planned change, the only change that is eventually acceptable to top management is that which they planned. And this in turn was based on conditions which existed *before* the plan was announced!"

(Gaffney, 2013, pgs. 390-391)

In describing Emergent change both Gaffney and Petersen are addressing phenomena of organisations which can be explained by the Field perspective. This has also arisen in science where Newtonian predictability has been replaced by the uncertainty of control found in quantum physics and models of complexity and Chaos theory.

Petersen offers several defining elements of complexity theory found in systems analysis and offers that complex systems are –

- *dynamic*, in that they change over time with previous states influencing and emerging into the next

- *non-linear* in that the effect is not predicable on the intensity and can be unforeseeable

- *show emergence*, in that through processes of self-organisation they create new and complex structures

To contrast these approaches of hierarchical and self-organised we have the following table from Petersen (adapted) -

	Hierarchical Management	Self-Organsied
General Orientation	Linear prediction and control	Non-linear complexity and emergence
Directions given	Clear goals and detailed instructions	Open-ended broad goals Operating from a sense of purpose
Achievements	Planned	Emergent
Use of general knowledge and abilities	Limited	Expansive
General problem solving capability	Not necessary	Necessary and possible
Control	External control	Internal self-regulation
Responsibility	Low	High
Interactions	Limited and top down. structured	Extensive, local, unstructured

The Paradox of Control – Gestalt Field Perspective

Gestalt therapy assimilates ideas of modern physics where observations influence the nature and identity of the observed and the observer. If you see service users as being demanding and self serving, you will treat them this way and you yourself may become cynical. If you see staff as being below you in a hierarchy, no matter how noble this may seem in your attitude, you will subtly treat them as below you and may become superior in your sense of self and attitude to them.

The paradoxical nature of reality described by gestalt therapy is similar to modern models of management attuned to complexity theory and self-organising systems. This correlation of gestalt therapy with the field theory of physics allows therapists to move beyond the individual, reductionist nature of most of psychology. Psychotherapy based on limited individualistic models views the therapist and client as two distinct entities. Field theory supports gestalt therapists in taking the step of being aware of the "self" of the therapist-client, the "self" of the couple, of the group and the community. This translates to management in which managers and staff affect one another - less like balls on a pool table and more like raindrops in a pond or lake – yet still with a clear sense of boundary like the pool balls. Perhaps a better analogy is one of magnets where they are clearly separate objects but their influence on one another in within an invisible magnetic field of which they are all a part. Each magnet affects the other.

This is similar a view offered in physics by Faraday in the 19th century. In a lecture in 1844 on the nature of atoms, Faraday made a bold leap of imagination and he turned the nature of reality away from the personal to the universal. He proposed that, rather than seeing atoms as physical objects which give of a web of force, perhaps the web of force itself was the reality and the atom existed as a concentration in that web of force. He then used a thought experiment to describe this, as a methodology.

He asked the audience to imagine the Sun sitting in space by itself. What would happen if the Earth suddenly appeared in its place? How would the Sun know it was there? He then said that before the Earth appeared the web of forces associated with the Sun – the field – is spread throughout space and so as soon as the Earth appeared it would have and impact on this field of force. This impact on the field would tell the Earth the Sun existed – therefore the Field is the reality the Earth experiences, not the Sun itself.

This is similar to the impact of a new CEO with an organisation. When people know she is starting work they already begin to be affected. Once she is there the impact she has as CEO extends well beyond the individual meetings with people. It lives in the invisible interactions in the wider field of influence, and through stories, gossip and other communication channels.

Faraday argued that these lines or webs of force filled the universe and is the reality by which these seemingly separate entities are connected - a field perspective. The material world of atoms and suns are like "knots" in the various fields of force. This is similar to the description which gestalt therapy offers of reality, self and organism-environment field. A simple example of this that helps to explain the self-organising and emergence affects between people in an organisation is found in a metaphor of a boat in Couples therapy. With a couple there is an invisible bond of the relationship which affects both the people – this is like a boat on a pond which they are both in – one person moves they move the other. When the therapist sees them for therapy they also affect and are affected by the couple as they are all in the boat together.

Similarly when someone joins an organisation, be they CEO, manager or new graduate, they all affect one another as they are in the boat (field) of the organisation. As this field affect is invisible, just like the gravitational field between planets, it is easy to believe and act "as if" it doesn't exist. However if the gravitational field altered or disappeared the disastrous impact would be felt immediately. While the person feels part of the organisation, like part of a solar system or boat on a lake, the affect of the organisation continues before and after our time at work. This is witnessed by sleepless nights of those worrying about work or the shift in the bond to a workplace as we prepare to leave – and sometimes people can pick up these subtle shifts if they are attuned to the field.

A Quantum of Control

As Einstein pointed out, the laws of quantum physics are statistical and therefore cannot measure or control an individual system (Uncertainty Principle) but instead a series of repeated measurements. This led him to believe that:

> *"Quantum physics deals only with aggregations, and its laws are for crowds and not for individuals"*
> *(Einstein and Infield 1938 p286)*

This implied that physicists must let go of the predictive control of classical Newtonian physics in deference to the statistical approximations of quantum physics. Likewise in Gestalt therapy, as opposed to other schools, we do not try to measure or "control" the individual as a separate phenomenon. Rather, we study the operation of the contact boundary in the organism/environment field. In line with Bohr, Gestalt therapy works with wholes. Earlier, non-field theorists talked about Gestalt therapy and the need for the therapist to exercise control of the therapeutic situation, often defined as "the therapist being able to persuade or compel the patient into following the procedures he has set" (Fagan and Shepherd, 1970, pp. 91-92)

More current theorists such as Hycner (1993) describe this as a paradoxical process of a searching for balance between choice and acceptance. This is perhaps best described in the original text of PHG as the "*middle mode*" of being - the space in between active and passive functioning, where the person is accepting, attending and growing into the solution. This is also the substitution of readiness (or faith) for the security of seeming control (Perls, Hefferline and Goodman, 1951; 1984 edition).

This is a key in expanding Contingency theory in management. If the manager is "attuned" to sense or intuit when to exert choice (and control) and when to accept and allow for self-organising emergence then contingency theory has shifted from an "either/or" to a "both/and" formulation – both hierarchical **and** self-organising rather than one or the other.

This allows managers to work from both aspects of a paradox – to hold a "both/and" perspective of reality. As a practical example, in teaching the field perspectives to therapists we show students "Magic Eye" books of pictures. They look like a jumbled chaos of colours from which, when they learn to soften and de-focus their gaze, a three dimensional image appears. The "trick" is to learn to look with "soft eyes" and out of chaos can appear harmony, with both "realities" being true for the observer.

In a similar way Bohm (1993) states the perceived classical world is a result of each mind, aware of only a small part of the whole. The illusory aspect is believing that this part IS the whole, as when we believe the jumble of colours is all there is, as that is all we are able to see. When the classical world is perceived as a facet, then there is no illusion. So as therapists as well as managers, the ability to "soften" our gaze to perceive other realities simultaneously becomes important. In a similar way, the issues raised of the need for governance and control of an organisation, as well as promoting the staff and the self-organisation of emergent change, have each their own validity within the frame of reference they arise from, depending on our gaze as manager.

From this perspective we manage from a contingency management space – and take what is useful from each management theory as long as we do not get caught up believing it is THE theory and practice.

The Paradox of Leadership

Management and organisational practices have been well articulated and cover various themes and situations. The defining in theory and practice of good leadership and how to achieve it is less apparent, if not somewhat esoteric. Roost (1991) argues there has been a continuing tendency to treat these words – management and leadership - as if they are synonymous which has been to the detriment of both ideas. Often leadership is subsumed within management and seen as the aspect or sub set of management processes which brings about a higher state of excellence, while management overall is "the rest".

Smircich and Morgan (1982) view leadership as the "management of meaning". They equate leadership to have occurred when one or more individuals succeed in framing or define the reality of others. To go further they say leadership may indeed have the *perceived* right and duty to do this. This equates to defining and sharing of roles and authority relationships within organisations that institutionalise the patterns of leadership.

They define this process of meaning-making using terms of "figure and ground" which causes me to wonder if they have been exposed to Gestalt psychology or gestalt therapy. Their process by which meaning-making occurs by leaders is as follows (adapted) -

Leadership: A figure-ground relationship which creates figure-ground relationships

Framing experience	Interpretation	Meaning and Action
Leadership action creates a focus of attention within the ongoing stream of experience which characterised the whole experience.	The action is interpreted within its wider context and the leader has a particular meaning in mind as they engage in action while others construct their own interpretation.	Action becomes grounded in the interpretation process the leader and others have engaged in

They critique this model of "meaning-making" based on the authority of the leader. They state that in doing so the leader may work against the development of staff in self responsibility, self initiative and self control - similar to critiques of bureaucracy. They argue that it is important to study and develop forms of "non-leadership" processes so adaptive abilities may develop at the level needed within the organisation.

In essence this approximates the process proposed by Plsek and Wilson (2010) in reviewing health service management in the UK, who propose advocating for the use of complexity theory in health service management. They argue that leadership inspired by complexity theory recognises that change occurs naturally within the system and that individuals engage in this effort for a variety of reasons. In this framework the leader's role is to create systems that disseminate rich information about better practices, allowing others to adapt those practices in ways that are most meaningful to them. This brings new ideas that provide fresh understandings of troubling issues in the organisation. Further management of delivery of health care and those who seek to change an organisation should harness the natural creativity and organising ability of its staff and stakeholders. This is through such principles as generative relationships, minimum specification and a constructive approach to variation in areas of practice where there is only moderate certainty and agreement.

As with Contingency theory, Complexity thinking accepts the paradox of variation as both potentially desirable and undesirable. For issues where there is a high degree of certainty about the result from an action, and a high degree of agreement among those who will take the action, then more controlled and directive approaches apply. At the same time when there is a successful variation from the norm or intuitive wisdom we need to study how variations in structure and process in the more successful hospitals contribute to variations in outcome. They note the biggest barrier to complexity and self-organising systems approaches are when there exist incumbent leaders of health systems who have risen within the hierarchy based on command and control methods. It is encouraging to note that the army, the stereotypical example of command and control leadership, is one of the pioneers in embracing new approaches based on complexity theory. As they state:

"If the military can successfully replace the field general with the facilitator, we have high hopes that the NHS can make a similar transition."

(Plsek, P.E. and Wilson, T. 2010, p. 749)

The challenges faced by being a manager and/or leader and knowing, guessing, or intuiting when to resort to more directive means and when to be open to the richer wisdom of the organisation and staff is akin to that of the gestalt therapist. This challenge is reiterated by Weymes (2004) who states:

"Today we cannot rely on one philosophical model to provide a framework for organisation design, since individual freedom must be tempered with bureaucratic controls"

(Weymes, 2004, pg. 343)

Weymes says traditionally, the CEO has focussed on the design and development of systems and processes while paying some attention to the "people" in the organisation. Today that focus must change so the people in the organisation control the systems and processes and not have the people controlled by the systems. While this sounds warm and fuzzy and even reasonable, one must remember that people as well as organisations are also attuned to their survival. This offers a continual challenge in this movement between relationship and survival, control and autonomy, bureaucracy and self-organising systems, modern and classical theory and the role a leader and manager is required to fulfil.

Emergent Change and Paradoxical Leadership

Both in modern management theory and gestalt therapy emergent change is a process whereby a figure emerges from the greater whole and is different and more than the sum of each part. This is a creative change from the field (organisation) without individual agency or intention on behalf of the leader– a holistic paradigm of creative change compared to a bureaucratic control of change in the organisation.

In essence, this equates to the agency of the whole towards the parts as aptly defined by Wertheimer previously when describing the field perspective in Gestalt psychology –

"There are wholes, the behavior of which is not determined by that of their individual elements, but where the part – processes are themselves determined by the intrinsic nature of the whole" (Wertheimer, 1925 in Ellis 1938, p. 2)

This principle in which a whole determines the behaviour of the individual parts is more usual than it might at first seem. It is prevalent in everyday life, where individuals are part of a team and they become swept into the synergy of the functioning of the team – such as with a sporting team, an orchestra or band, a choir, a emergency team in a hospital, a family and community. Even with individual pursuits in arts, theatre, sports, and drama, the combined experience of the performer and the audience can come together to create an experience (or figure) which emerges creatively from the whole and is not dependant on the performer. In therapy this creative process as a figure which emerged from the field of the implicit reality (or implicate order) of the client/therapist field (O'Neill & Gaffney, 2008) and is co-created by both client and therapist. Thus also in the field of management the emergent change is co-created by the leader, the staff and the organisation as a whole pre-eminently.

The idea and principles guiding practices of a leader/manager from such a model of emergent change are challenging to new and old managers alike. To accept and work as a manager from this principle of emergent creation needs a degree of surrender by the leader and staff as well as the organisation as whole. O'Neill and Gaffney (2008) title this "surrender to paradoxical agency" and describe how in Gestalt therapy, as opposed to other schools, we do not try to measure or "control" the individual as a separate phenomenon and this also equates to such work in management and leadership.

The field perspective consists of being aware and attuned to the operation of field (organisation) rather than satisfying the need for the manager to exercise control of the organisation as in some approaches. That is easier said than done of course, particularly for a new manager who is doing their best to apply the theory to practice, and therefore "trying" to exert some form of control over what is happening. Also as previously stated this is an even bigger ask for leaders who have risen within the hierarchy based on command and control methods

In part, the challenge of allowing and working with emergent creation is a paradoxical process of searching for balance between wilful choice and acceptance of what "is" for the manager, staff and organisation. This is described in the original Gestalt therapy text of Perls et al (1951) as the *middle mode* – the space between active and passive functioning, where the person is accepting, attending and growing into the solution, with the substitution of readiness (or faith) for the security of apparent control (Perls, Hefferline and Goodman, 1951).

The original text of Perls et al (1951) when applied to management and leadership asks managers, from a field perspective, to have faith in something more than the leader's individual agency - to let go of their need for security and control and instead be present in the moment – to be present to the emergent creation of change in the organisation field.

This *"readiness"* of middle mode described by Perls et al (1951) offers a paradoxical agency or control – an ability to sense and chose being "in control" by relinquishing control. They equate this state to one which is more familiar to children and artists, and indeed examples of such paradoxical agency are found aplenty in the arts, music and poetry, such as in the work of William Wordsworth. It is also a state frequently referred to by people who describe spiritual experiences, such a Martin Buber. What follows is a description of how such a process is taught to therapists in Gestalt therapy as described by O'Neill (2008). This may also be considered as showing practices and keys to become open to the emergent change within an organisation when developed beyond the therapy frame.

Poetic Practice in Gestalt Therapy Training

It is the task of the trainer and supervisor to envisage ways to create a setting which, though structured, provides the safety and stage in which the trainee can justifiable let go a little of the need for control and allow themselves to be in the moment. One such exercise developed in training at the Illawarra Gestalt Centre has been borrowed from work with Frank Farrelly and Steve Brigham. It has three steps or stages. Trainees begin by sitting in dyads and we explore first how each person prepares themselves so as to be less distracted and more present. The first experience then involves one person taking the time to be in a state where they feel ready and then at this point they signal the other person to begin talking. As the second person talks the "job" of the first person is to sit silently attuned to the other.

This first part is usually very challenging as students who are being silent and centred want to indicate in all variety of ways that they are, indeed, attending and so some vigorously nod and gesticulate in order to do so. The result, as they discuss afterwards, is that paradoxically such concerns reduce their sense of being present, both for them and the other person. Yet this now offers the student and practitioner an awareness of being *as* doing, and not needing to do for the sake of doing.

The next step in the experience is for the silent person to now talk when they want to and to allow this to emerge from whatever takes their own fancy, irrelevant to the person opposite them. Therefore as an example the trainer may display how to talk gobbildy-gook and speak in word salad.

This experience is freeing for some and alternatively unbearable for others who hold a need to be the "good attentive" therapist and once again, when discussed afterwards, brings fruitful discussions around the balance of excessively attending versus relaxing into a spontaneous space.

The final phase of the experience involves the person now being centred and present, as well as sensing their ability to be spontaneous, and using this therapeutically. The spontaneous responses which are invited are the various images which arise for the therapist. They are thus able to practice being spontaneous therapeutically by sharing whatever images come into their head while the other person talks. They are encouraged to trust in the image and share it (and not further explain it) for the other person. The result is that they experience these images arising spontaneously and outside their ego control, and the person talking begins to make meaning from the images. As with reflective listening, the images may be altered by the person talking and that is also encouraged as a co-created field. One might say "as you talk about your work, I get the sudden image of a cage" and the person may say "well it is but I am aware the door of the cage is open."

This experience also brings both therapist and client outside of "talking about" the issues and more actively accessing a richer language of experience of imagery, similar to that of poetry. In such moments the barrier of talk can dissolve into mutuality between the two people.

Application to Management and Leadership

These exercises help develop practical skills of being more open to creative change and paradoxical control. They are also applicable to the management and leadership setting in an organisation. Petersen notes that a "good spirit" in management can bring out an energy and result greater than the sum of the energy put in and that this not achieved by "mindless" management but by a leadership attuned to the people and the organisation. It involves taking the risks of giving and sharing power to those with the proper know how and direct experience of the work, and creating conditions that allow people to "plan, control, organise and coordinate their work". I have found this necessary in a leadership role where I am responsible for other managers in a team. This did not mean surrendering authority or direction or whatever, and came more from an attitude that trusted others to be able to do the work and at the same time being attuned and open to when they needed support, advice or supervision - providing direction and focus without prescribing the exact route to take.

In the next section of the book we consider the various parts, principles and practices of Gestalt therapy and their practical application to work as a manager and leader.

Gestalt Therapy: An Overview

Introduction: The Gestalt Hologram
A Methodology for Integrating Theory and Practice

To help explain a complex process such as Gestalt therapy we have developed a model of training and supervision (O'Neill & O'Neill, 2008) which we call the *Gestalt Hologram*. This developed over thirty years of training Gestalt therapists and draws on three main sources. The first of these is *Profound Simplicity* as described by Will Schutz who developed the Encounter Group.

Profound Simplicity

Will Schutz describes the process of learning as that of discovering *Profound Simplicity* (wisdom) out of a complexity of ideas, (Schutz, 1979). He proposed there are three stages in understanding a phenomenon. To explain this we use the metaphor of a forest and its complexity.

The first is the *simplistic view* – a forest is a forest is a forest - a collection of trees. In entering the forest and delving deeper along its many paths, the complexity of the forest becomes apparent. What unfolds is its nature as a dense web of life where rare lichen may grow in the specific temperature, light and moisture.

This second stage of learning Schutz calls the *complex view*. At this stage our logical brains can easily become overwhelmed by so much data, struggling to bring together the connections within chaos into a meaningful pattern or harmonic.

The final stage of learning is where eventually as we leave the forest and look back, we view the forest as a whole again. Yet unlike the first stage where this view is simple, this view is one which is *profoundly simple* and includes the complexity within the simplicity.

When we get there at times, we can rest, take it in, celebrate – and then return to the chaos of the complexity!

David Bohm and the Hologram

David Bohm worked with Einstein and became Professor of Theoretical Physics at London University. In his book *The Undivided Universe* (Bohm, 1993) he offers a metaphor from quantum physics which translates to psychotherapy - the hologram. The hologram produces a three-dimensional image by splitting and reunifying light, and offers a model for both how the brain "creates" reality and how each *part* of a reality contains the *whole*. What interested Bohm was the hologram does not look like the object it projects but creates an image when it is illuminated. What was most of interest to us in teaching Gestalt therapy was how to teach the "bits" each session while preserve a connection and awareness of the "whole", particularly with a topic such as Gestalt therapy which can become so complex.

Philosophy, Principle and Practice

The third influence in developing the Gestalt Hologram was the importance in training and practice for the practice of therapy to be ethical and not just rote or copied or mimicked. Thus our practice must of necessity be guided by the core principles of our work and these arise out of the personality theory and philosophical ground from which they spring, which includes research and studies of outcome. Our training model works from the premise the *PRACTICE* of counselling and psychotherapy are developed from underlying *PRINCIPLES* which in turn arise from *PERSONALITY* theory which in turn is nourished and developed from a *PHILOSOPHY* or world view (figure 1.)

PHILOSOPHY

I

PERSONALITY THEORY

I

PRINCIPLES

I

PRACTICE

The Gestalt Hologram Model has been used as a teaching tool in the Illawarra Gestalt Centre since the early 1990's. The idea of the Gestalt Hologram was to capture a profoundly simple *gestalt* or map of Gestalt therapy and we found the hologram is a useful metaphor as in a *hologram each part contains the whole*, yet is *also a part by itself*.

This principle of a hologram is what underlies the model. The main philosophical aspect of Gestalt therapy which is central to the therapy is that of the field perspective. This is manifested in the other philosophical elements of gestalt therapy which other writers have described as key pillars—namely phenomenology, dialogue/existentialism and behaviourism.

These elements show the Profound Simplicity of the therapy. They are a guide and a compass to "find our way home" to the core values, attitudes and practices of the psychotherapy work.

These elements of Gestalt therapy are displayed pictorially as holographic "spaces" on the two dimensions of the diagram, where each space defines the key Philosophy, the key Principle and the key Practice of that aspect of Gestalt therapy. The important thing to remember in looking at each of these elements is that *they also contain all the other elements at the same time.*

Therefore the picture of the Hologram shows the separate elements or pillars of Gestalt therapy yet you must also imagine holographically each "part" also contains the whole, and by being able to look at it as a whole unit you can in essence "see" Gestalt therapy at a glance. This allows the whole and its parts to exist pictorially for the student in a way that is replicated in teaching modules of gestalt therapy and then bringing them together holistically in practice.

As well as providing a profoundly simple pictorial map of Gestalt therapy, this simple hologram model is used to support the process of the training and supervision (O'Neill & O'Neill, 1995).

Gestalt Hologram

(O'Neill & O'Neill, 1995 & 2008)

Phenomenology

Awareness

"Here and now "

Dialogue/Existentialism

Contact/relationship

"I - thou"

Field theory

Connectedness

"Authentic self"

Behaviourism

Experiment

"What and how"

In the following chapters we will now outline each of these component parts and their application in management and leadership - Phenomenology (Awareness); Dialogue (Relationship) and Behaviourism (Experiment).

Phenomenology and Management:
Philosophy, Principles and Practice

Philosophy

Phenomenology was an important movement of the early 20th century. Its basic tenet is that all knowledge is subjective and therefore cannot be considered apart from the mind doing the "knowing" and it has been incorporated into much of modern culture including psychology and therapy. Gestalt therapy as an existential psychotherapy draws inspiration from Heidegger and those who followed in his path. (Bloom, 2008)

Gestalt psychology noticed the interaction of figure and ground to make meaning was also obvious even in our visual field as in these two famous gestalt pictures:

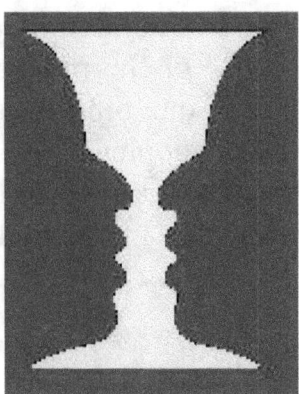 

In the following picture our senses tell us the two circles are of different sizes when they are the same, however our "reality" is also affected by the context of the figure or the ground (in this case the size of the other circles.)

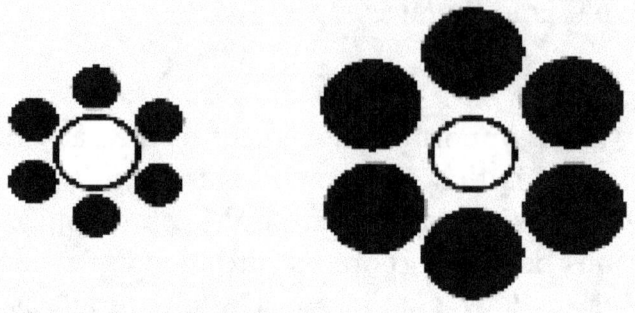

Fritz Perls (1966) provides a profoundly simple answer to the question of what is phenomenology in the form of a metaphorical equation:

now = experience = awareness = reality

Principles

In teaching Gestalt therapy it helps to be able to find acronyms and simple devices to help us learn the "bits" of the process before it finally sinks in and become a part of our repertoire. Various authors in gestalt therapy define the phenomenological method in approximately the same way and to assist students we have developed what are the main principles in a simple acronym.

Key components of the phenomenological method
- *Bracketing*
- *Interest*
- *Insight*
- *Naive view*
- *Discrimination*

As this method is about not getting into the bind of *believing* that what we *assume* we see is what we *actually* see, we can remember it by the acronym of B.I.I.N.D.

Bracketing
Interest
Insight
Naive view
Discrimination

Bracketing:

Bracketing is being aware of your ability to create the reality we see - thus knowing I will create you in my experience and not just observe you. This offers the opportunity to discriminate between what is imagined and what is observable and felt. To assist developing skills in bracketing it helps to discriminate our awareness into three zones -

- Outer Zone
- Inner Zone
- Middle Zone

Outer zone:
Awareness of what is external to the person – what can be seen, tasted, heard, smelt and touched.
Inner zone:
Awareness of what is internal for the person – body sensations, feelings, proprioception, movement.
Middle zone:
Awareness of what is "between" inner and outer – what is imagined, fantasied, thought and assumed.
These zones of awareness can be used to help discriminate between observed and imagined experiences. For example if

someone in giving a lecture they may consider two possible realities:

Outer Zone	Inner Zone	Middle Zone
Aware of people looking at me as I'm about to speak on stage	Awareness of tingling in my body and of my breathing	I imagine they think I don't know much and I am anxious

Outer Zone	Inner Zone	Middle Zone
Aware of people looking at me as I'm about to speak on stage	Awareness of tingling in my body and of my breathing	I imagine I'm excited and ready to connect with them

Interest

The concept of bracketing supports the therapist and client to explore and experiment with what is reality and how they co-create it As therapists we develop an interest and respect for the person's experience knowing for example that they are the expert on their experience as this is their experiencing - even if they are "wrong" as judged by outsiders - as outsiders cannot fully experience how and why they experience what they do.

Insight:

Insight is the meaning we give to a figure in relation to the ground - the figure is given meaning when we see it in the ground it arises in. This includes the ground of past experiences which shape how we view now. Phenomenological inquiry is finding out about the clients ground and how it gives meaning to the figure. So as a therapist we start to understand why the client might feel depressed at the thought of Christmas dinner. Phenomenological inquiry is to begin to see the world from the others perspective and naively explore how they perceive the world.

Naive View:

To naively explore how the client perceives the world. Therefore what is "subjective" and what is "objective" are equally valid from this approach. The "naive" experience is to be able to describe rather than explain and start with equal value to all observations.

Discrimination:

Discrimination is being aware of and exploring the difference between our *observed* reality and that of our *imagined* reality with assumptions - discriminating between past and present, between residual/current experiences: a movement of our awareness from what is IMAGINED to what is IMMEDIATE which is in essence being aware of here and now experiences.

The following diagrams use the Hologram to provide a simple guide to map the shift to between immediate and imagined.

Imagined

Awareness   Relationship
There and Then   *Them and It*

Experiment
Why why why

Immediate

Awareness   Relationship
Here and Now   *I -Thou*

Experiment
What and How

Awareness and "Here and Now"

A central idea of gestalt therapy is awareness brings change. Out of awareness change occurs spontaneously Most of us, at some point in our lives, have learned to avoid awareness of certain parts of ourselves and of our experience, avoiding frightening or unpleasant feeling. Gestalt Therapy involves expanding your awareness so you know more about yourself. It is often convenient to distinguish different areas of awareness. Awareness without systematic exploration is not normally enough to develop insight; therefore, Gestalt therapy uses focused awareness and experimentation to achieve insight. Phenomenology applied to Management

As stated previously, Petersen (2007) argues that modern management theory has become like a house of mirrors in a carnival which shows distorted pictures of reality. He talks of the change noticed in the Health services in Britain which shifted from seeing service users as needy to being demanding and complaining. Such a shift will bring many changes to the Health Service Industry and will of course affect both the service users and the service providers in how they relate to and understand each other. The cause of change in behaviours and attitudes by service users may be that as Health Services become more economically rationalist and work to reduce costs (and staff etc) the actual "service" may of course become reduced with longer waiting times, diversions to other hospitals, patients left on trolleys in hallways. The list goes on and appears common in many Western world facilities today. Until this is explored and our view of reality is expanded, as staff we might easily continue to deal with the "front line" and not see to the deeper meaning of why service users are upset and they may simply see staff as rude or rushed. And of course the media play a part in this and the way in which these realities are interpreted and "constructed". For the viewers watching the News this forms a view of hospitals as only being this one way. Fortunately other stories appear (and TV programs) which present the other side of this story where dedicated workers and thankful patients are seen.

In applying the phenomenological method to management we begin by realising we do not know the realities of the staff or the organisation situation as much as might think we do. It is not until we are open and willing **bracket** what we *assume and think* are the answers, that we can see beyond these partial and 'personal perspective' truths to the other truths that exist beyond us. Once we start from a place where we know our truth and perspective is clearly not the only one, then we are beginning the first step of being phenomenological as managers. This first step leads us to have an **interest** in just what might be the view and perspective of other, which also eventually trains us to take a more **naive** and open attention so as not to keep assuming we know. Eventually as we and others embark on this phenomenological exploration, the way people make meaning of their situation and experience provide us and them **insight** about why and how we make such meaning, and thus have the possibility to distinguish and **discriminate** between various possibilities about what the reality is and how we colour that with our perspective.

In one such instance I was asked to consult with a Federal department which dealt with the unemployed and paying unemployment benefits. There were two groups of staff - those who stood at the front counter and dealt direct with unemployed people and those who sat in the offices behind them doing computer and office work. I had assumed that conflict in the teams was because of the counter staff enduring the stress of the direct customer service compared with the staff in the back-office. At first inquiry there was some truth in this but it did not hit the bullseye so I inquired further. What eventuated was front counter staff were annoyed and disgruntled with one another. At first this made no sense to me as I had imagined they would be "sisters in arms" against the sheltered backroom staff.

When the back-office staff did not help out - well they were just back-office staff, what could you expect of them? The undisclosed issue they had been sitting on was it was the real bone of contention. When a counter staff person would step out to go to the toilet and take a five-minute break and cigarette -

well that was the greatest of sins - they should know better and know the load that placed on the other counter staff.

Once this became clear and I could understand and have more insight to their issue I suggested and alternative work practice. This was a subtle shift in this strong bond of working the counter. I explored with them that if they didn't do this how else they could get a break to help them avoid abusing customers or breaking down in tears. Might it not be good to step back for a moment? This would be a sign of them looking after one another (and the complaint was that they weren't) and were doing so now with choice and not in shamed or secretive way. And since they were doing it anyway might it not be better if they all agreed, in awareness, that not only was it a good thing to "take five" but this was another way they could strengthen their work bond and support one another consciously? Their faces were alight with delight.

The success of this intervention in a workplace in the end belonged to these workers of course. My role was a being in a process of not knowing, finding out and suggesting how to experiment with other ways of seeing the same thing. If they did not chose to do this or wanted to stay stuck with being annoyed then there would not be the delight and we would need to continue by exploring why they still felt stuck. This is the potency of the phenomenological method. It is that as long as a manager is on a continuous journey of finding out then they will not stay stuck with thinking they know all the answers. This counters the view that they **should** know all the answers as they are in charge, the manager, the leader.

As mentioned before Smircich and Morgan (1982) view leadership as the "management of meaning" when one or more individuals succeed in framing or define the reality of others. In one model this management of meaning was viewed as the role of the leader/manager and this is seen in Classical and Neo-classical theories of management. More modern theorists, particularly those favouring Culture and Complexity views of management promote the manager and leader as being willing to create systems that *expand* meaning. This honours the wider views within and outside the organisation while still having the flexibility to lead in a directive or visionary way when suitable.

Dialogical Aspects of Management

While the phenomenological method focuses on what is manifestly "observed" phenomenon of individuals, the dialogical approach extends to include inner reality and the connection that exists between people as they share their inner and outer reality. Maurice Nichols, a British neurologist in the mid 20th century, was a student of Gurjief. He described how when people meet there are two "realities" – the visible and the invisible.

There is a world not visible to others which only the person can experience. As they think, feel, imagine and even dream, no-one else can be aware of this unless it is shared. This is our private invisible world. When we then look at another person we realise that they too have access to this invisible reality in themselves. Therefore most of what we see and hear is not the whole person. We don't have access to their invisible world unless they tell us about it. This invisible world includes feelings and thoughts, love and wisdom. Therefore most of what is important in life and is all around us - is this invisible inner world. The awareness of this inner "essential" world of self and the external world of "observed" phenomenon is crucial understanding the dialogical philosophy of Martin Buber.

Melnick (1997) describes the shift from Freud to present day psychotherapy where therapeutic focus moved from *within* (intrapsychic) to *between* (interpersonal), and from *understanding* to *feeling*. The goal of therapy also broadened, from the uncovering of neuroses to the working through of issues of intimacy and connection. Simultaneously, the role of the therapist changed from that of a scientific and detached clinician to an authentic, transparent, emotional, and at times, self-disclosing therapist. He notes how the development of Gestalt therapy was heavily influenced by the work of Otto Rank and by the dialogical approach of Buber (1958). It demands a willingness of two or more individuals to be open in a broad and deep way to the other's experience.

Philosophy – Principle - Practice

Philosophy
A dialogic existentialist approach is based on Martin Buber who saw two ways of being in the world: "I -It "(seeing people as objects) and "I-thou"(discovering the connectedness). In therapy this involves engaging the therapist and the client experiencing the other person as he/she is - showing the true self and sharing phenomenological awareness. Gestalt dialogue embodies authenticity and responsibility

> "The therapist does not.... rest on the broad upland of system that includes a series of sure statements about the absolute, but on a narrow, rocky ridge between the gulfs where there is no sureness of expressible knowledge but the certainty of meeting what remains undisclosed."
>
> Buber (1965, pg.184)

Principles of Dialogical Therapy
1. Presence
2. Inclusion
3. Commitment to dialogue
4. Non exploitative stance
5. Dialogue is lived

1. Presence
The therapists own experience and phenomenology are available - they express observations, preferences, feelings, personal experience as part of the therapeutic relationship.

100

Thus the therapist can share his perspective by modeling phenomenological reporting by aiding the client's learning about the trust and use of immediate experience to raise awareness

2. Inclusion

The therapist includes herself in the world of the client while upholding her own sense of self. This is putting oneself as fully as possible into the experience of the other, without judging or interpreting, while simultaneously keeping a sense of one's separateness. Inclusion is the back and forth movement of being centered in one's own existence and yet being able to go over to the "other side".

3. Commitment to dialogue

The surrender to an interpersonal process, *allowing* contact to happen between *rather than controlling* the contact and the outcome

4. Non exploitative stance

Influencing or adjusting to the goal of the client and protecting the integrity of the person's actual experience
Not treating the person as an "It" but as a "Thou"

5. Dialogue is lived

Dialogue is "lived" emphasizes the excitement and immediacy of living rather than only reporting about it alone or talking "about" without also expressing directly to the other.

Skilled Crafted Responses – The Ethics of the Dialogical Approach

Melnick et al. (1994), in their work on ethics and Gestalt therapy, talk about the Gestalt therapist having difficulty with the "intimate moments" of interpersonal work as opposed to the traditional insight oriented approach of the Freudian school. They describe four ethical transgressions which can arise and how to avoid such transgressions when working from a dialogical frame.

- the therapist states too much too soon for the client
- the therapist speaks from their own ethical base and fails to acknowledge when their values are different from the clients
- an over emphasis on one of the polarities of dependency-independence
- the therapist is unable to tolerate the client's expression of emotion and looks to a quick fix or avoiding the client when the client is expressing strong feelings at the therapist

These are replaced by skilled crafted responses –

- To be able to stay with the client while the client experiences intense emotional states.
- To balance therapist contact and presence attuned to the client
- To manage dependence – independence
- To be willing to speak from their own ethical values and beliefs while also acknowledging the client's

Dialogical Management

As with phenomenology, the dialogical approach can extend to management practice without the therapeutic aspects which have been described. The phenomenological aspects of management help ensure the manager and leader can better understand staff, the organisation and the field of work they find themselves. Dialogue adds an authentic, personal fullness for the manager and leader, particularly in their role as leader.

Using the metaphor of the Sun, the phenomenological approach may be equated to the light from the sun - the vision and clarity that is required from a leader and ability to encourage others to shed their light in the work. Dialogue in this metaphor can be equated to the heat from the sun - the will, motivation and feeling the manager and leader bring to the job that not only inspires other but helps them in shaping their motivation.

Plsek and Wilson (2010) see management and leadership in modern theory working with complexity theory. This combines both motivational/relationship elements as well as those that are phenomenological. They argue the science of complex adaptive systems brings new concepts that provide fresh understandings of troubling issues in the organisation and management of delivery of health care. Effective organisation and delivery of health care does not need detailed targets and specifications, nor should it focus primarily on controlling the process or overcoming resistance -

> "Rather, those who seek to change an organisation should harness the natural creativity and organising ability of its staff and stakeholders through such principles as generative relationships, minimum specification, the positive use of attractors for change, and a constructive approach to variation in areas of practice where there is only moderate certainty and agreement."
>
> (Plsek, P.E. and Wilson, T. 2010, p. 749)

103

Therefore generative relationships and positive use of attractors encourage leaders using the dialogical relational aspects of management as well as those that are phenomenological, such as specifications and understanding variations.

In the two previous examples I gave of the staff member who thought we just wanted to get rid of her and the manager who thought the rest of the management team were against her, I found my dialogical experience as a therapist was invaluable. As a manager it involves in those instances my being able to stay with the process and share my self and my motivations (**Presence)** while knowing I was not in charge of the outcome (**Commitment).** At the same time I made the effort to not only understand the person but to try and put myself in their position and how this felt for them (**Inclusion**). While I was hoping for a good outcome for the organisation I had decided to put the welfare of the person into the equation to be **Non-exploitive.** As both people knew me I believe they knew this is how I **lived** and was not just a management manipulation.
Building Trust

The Dialogical approach to management however is not solely for interactions between two individuals as with the therapist and client in counselling. It has a broader impact within modern management theory. Weymes (2004) notes this shift in attention to relationships in the wider organisation culture and milieu and the challenge this creates for leaders and managers -

> "Today the chief executive is challenged with the task of building trust and integrity in the organisation. When trust pervades the organisation there is commitment from the staff and support from the external community. Trust is based on shared values and value systems lie at the heart of human behaviour,

behaviour that cannot be controlled through systems and processes, the traditional operating standard for many organisations. If corporate social responsibility is vested in gaining the trust of stakeholders, inside and outside the organisation, then the fundamental philosophy must be based on the organisation's ability to build relationships.

Relationships are established between people and cannot be mandated by strict adherence to systems and processes. The people within the organisation must subscribe to the values of the organisation and those outside the organisation must admire those values. The organisation must be values driven. Thus the organisation that espouses corporate social responsibility must develop an environment where people in the organisation work together in a harmonious manner and external stakeholders form an emotional connection with the organisation while keeping its commitment to the financial investors"

(Weymes, 2004 pp. 349)

When I was working with Relationships Australia I met Peter Langford from Macquarie University whom had oversight of our staff survey process through what is termed "The Voice Project". This surveys, in particular, engagement, leadership and service quality. At that time they had surveyed over 2,500 organisations and over half a million staff. While measuring such concepts as engagement and leadership are complex there are several profound simplicities they present which are worth considering.

One of the interesting findings is that senior leaders in the organisation have a bigger impact than supervisors or program co-ordinators, which at first is counter-intuitive. While for some functions of course delegation is essential, they have found that "relationship management" must be a core part of the role of leaders and senior managers. Further while there are variances across sectors and industries there are more similarities than differences. The attributes for effective leaders they have surveyed are –

- vision
- advocacy
- supporting and recognising others
- optimism

An additional process, which I would argue is another attribute, is that of communication – good leaders need to communicate. Langford argues that the reason communication is so important is it meets a wide variety of human needs –

- reminding people of their purpose and importance
- making them feel involved
- help them feel a part of the group
- recognising their efforts and achievements
- developing knowledge
- increase awareness
- show they have been heard
- and to show the leader can both understand and empathise

If we consider these in relation to the Gestalt Hologram there are aspects which fit with each of the areas. Some, such as understanding and caring apply to two areas and thus again demonstrate the nature of holographic reality.

Phenomenology (awareness)
- reminding people of their purpose
- developing knowledge
- increase awareness
- and to show the leader can both understand and empathise

Dialogue (relationship)
- reminding people of their importance
- making them feel involved
- help them feel a part of the group
- recognising their efforts and achievements
- show they have been heard
- and to show the leader can both understand and empathise

Experiment
- recognising their efforts and achievements

As these aspects all form part of the central principle of the Field Perspective in gestalt therapy, I would consider this the core area which unites them all. With the Field Perspective the Principle is *Connectedness* and the Practice is *Authentic Self*. This holographic perspective is a *"unified field theory"* of the attributes of a leader – the authentic leader or manager.

Equating trust and engagement connect theoretically and trust is built with staff and they feel engaged when the leaders show the sort of attributes means staff can trust their manager. I have experienced developing trust and respect to be dependent on a genuine willingness to work collaboratively, accept a wide range of views and to provide a relationship which is authentic and dependable. This will be developed further in its own chapter as we explore what it is to be authentic as a leader and manager.

Dialogical Aspects of the Manger Role: Supervision, grievance and complaints

We read earlier of the skilled crafted responses of the counsellor or therapist in keeping the dialogical relationship in the therapeutic setting. These principles can be transposed to workplace, in areas such as supervision, staff grievances and complaints. These principles offered guidance when working in difficult situations where emotions start to run high, particularly where conflict between staff or with staff and management arises. In such cases most organisations have policies and procedure which direct or guide the manager, yet these by themselves are logical or "right brain". When the interpersonal relationships being managed become emotional the logic and phenomenological clarity of the policy and procedure can quickly become overrun by high emotionality. In such cases managers and human resource people are often, as with counselling, taken by surprise by the emotional intensity. Their first mistakes may be similar to those of the counsellor in a similar situation –

- The manager states too much too soon for the staff member or members

This can take the form of telling staff "how it's going to be" or explaining to them why they are doing what they do or outlining the policy and procedures etc. This of course does not get through the emotionality of the staff members. Staff then feel unheard and unventilated - which works against a solution and the emotions either are stored up or burst forth more.

- The manager speaks from their own ethical base and fails to notice when their values are different from the staff member or members.

In this situation it becomes a lecture to staff members on how they are meant to be and act at work - what is expected of them and even worse resorting to reading out the position description. This will not allow for opening of the communication and phenomenological inquiry. Instead managers want to understand the whole issue which is "what does the staff member or members feel and think about this – how it makes sense from their perspective?"

- An overemphasis on one of the polarities of dependency-independence

Under situations of high emotional intensity and conflict in the workplace the less experienced manager may feel the need to step up and step in and take charge. This has the result of disabling the people involved and not allowing them to take responsibility for what is happening. In the process this again also potentially intensifies the emotions.

- The manager cannot tolerate the staff's expression of emotion and looks to a quick fix or avoiding the staff member (s) when they are expressing strong feelings at the manager.

In such cases there is reduction to hear what is happening and how people are feeling and thinking. While abusive reactions need not be tolerated, staff may also cry, feel depressed, and feel like giving up. All such emotions need to be heard by the manager. If this feels beyond the current competence of the manager, other people may need to be used such as mediators. The antidotes to these dialogical errors are as follows –

- To be able to stay with the staff member(s) while they experiences intense emotional states.
- To balance manager's contact and presence attuned to the staff member(s).
- To manage dependence – independence
- To be willing to speak from their own ethical values and beliefs while also acknowledging the staff member(s).

These skills do not come easy - some managers who are not counsellors or therapists do have a natural ability which is to be applauded. For those who do not or come from a non-dialogical space the secret is this is easier to learn than it might seem. Practice, practice and practice are clear indicators for success and the use of a mentor/supervisor is invaluable. In the next chapter we will explore this in considering the principles that guide an authentic manager from the Field perspective.

The Authentic Leader and Manager

One of the constant, enduring and challenging issues of being a manager is deciding the proper contact and relationship with others in the workplace.

The Role of the Manager

As a therapist and manager every day I am called on to negotiate the space between myself and others in complex fields. There are times when I find that I am acting almost totally within the role of manager, like any other manager, without any recourse to, awareness of or sense of my training as a Gestalt therapist. For example, when I am completing a monthly finance and business report I find little if any use for Gestalt therapy. There are many times when working as a manager needs specific skills which are non-relational and not related to therapy. Of course there are also times when managers are required to be relational, and there is significant management theory and principles already developed from social sciences which inform this. The application of one's skill when the manager is a therapist would seem a natural progression.

The Genesis of the Therapist/Manager

When I started managing teams I was also working as a clinician. I tended to see tasks as "management" and others as "clinical". However once I became mainly a manager I found my skills as a manager predominated and even need going against what I might do as a therapist, for example in a disciplinary interview.

Over time having developed some degree of mastery in management, the usefulness of my therapy skills seemed to return. As examples, I remember an occasion where a staff member had a grievance with another manager who reported to me. We were meeting with personnel and unions to sort this out. The staff member glared at me and blurted out

"You just want me to leave and have no problems! That would be easier for everyone"

I knew as a manager my job was to "manage" this and craft a reply which followed policy and procedure and implicitly protected the organisation.

Yet something of the therapist in me stepped forward and I said

"Well part of me does and yet part of me does not, and I imagine part of you just wants to kick at us as an organisation because you feel you've been treated badly. I also imagine there is part of you which wants to work this out."

"I also believe if I just let you resign, not only would that not work for you, but it would be wrong for me also"

I sensed the personnel manager's virtual apoplexy as we waited for a reply.

"Yes, you're right" the staff-member said.

From this position we could negotiate to help her return to a team which had rallied against her in support of the manager and continue the dialogue among all concerned. I sensed a choice point in this, which is even clearer in hindsight, where she and I and later the other manager and team, could be aware of our tendencies as a human being to either fight or dialogue with each other. We had choices, which originally were more implicit and hidden, but which being made explicit, shifted the field.

In another example I was a manager for a team of twelve managers, some of whom worked for non-government organisations and were managed by our bureaucracy. We were developing not only as a work group but with the intention of being a team. I had described the Gestalt approach to utilising the group as a whole and the managers were open to this as they had therapy backgrounds.

One of the managers felt that her service, which was politically powerful, was purposely being ostracised by the other services and as she talked about this she became tearful and angry and was about to leave. I also imagined she felt embarrassed at this.

I realised this was an important moment which could affect the possible development, or deconstruction, of team as a whole in how she was received or not. I still remember that an aspect of myself, which I am more used to in a therapy setting, loomed large. I said "Well not only do I hear what you say, I also notice at some level you can say all this here, and I'm glad that you do."
While she cried a little more her anger disappeared and she forcefully told us this issue had been painful as this was an important group for her and she wanted this to work. Her clear statement and the authentically warm response she received from the others was a key step in this group of managers working together as a team. She was welcomed as part of the team and a dialogue began.

Years later I learnt from a colleague (Lee 2004) that we can promote an ethical field of connectedness, or belonging, where the relationships themselves encourage and support ethical, authentic behaviours between people. Yet at the time, my response was a reflex as a Gestalt therapist to value dialogue and authentic relationships - to realise everyone is influenced by dark and light, yin and yang. Once we are more aware of this we can choose between the dark and light, between relationship and survival. I value as a therapist the therapeutic alliance and the possibility for the paradoxical theory of change to come into play.

Paradoxical Theory of Change

The paradoxical nature of change is exemplified in difficult areas of management such as complaints, grievances and disciplinary processes. For some managers, if not most, this is an area where the more logical and linear processes of planning and strategy go awry. The normal movement forward to achieve goals becomes disrupted by an oppositional force which tends in the opposite direction. This may cause a manager to pull in the opposite direction and the staff member may be seen as "oppositional" or "not up to standard" - needing performance management and disciplinary procedures. While these tried and tested methods of attending to performance are necessary and useful, it is also of benefit to a manager to work in a paradoxical way. As described in the case example above, the principle which guides this from a gestalt therapy perspective is to accept the polarities in the field and understand each polarity has something to offer in someway.

Such an approach may need, at times, the "patience of a saint" however the reward as described in the case examples above is a less oppositional process with a wider inclusion of the context

114

of the complaint, grievance or performance issues. Further there are wider choices available for a manager and staff member other than the "High Noon" of deciding to terminate an employee.

One consultant offering a training workshop mentioned the 20-60-20 model. 20% of employees are not engaged and need to move on, 20% are forging ahead by themselves and the most return will come from working with the 60%. A different metaphor is that of a garden shop. Plants may not be doing well because they are in the shaded cool parts of the shop and need to be moved to the sun. Others in the sun need to be in the humid hot house. Sometimes an employee does not need to leave but may benefit from moving to another part of the work place or to a different or adjusted job configuration. These "shifts" may also be internal shifts of attitude and thinking and this applies to the manager as well as the employee. The manager, from a dialogical and field perspective, is clearly in some way part of this process and may "own" more of the complaint and performance issue that at first may be obvious. In this vein I sometimes mention to others managers the story of Buddha's cook.

Buddha's Cook - A Counterintuitive Reflex

This is one of the stories which help assess a situation and find meaning and direction to what at first instincts and emotional reaction offer only one view. Once I feel ONLY one way about a management I issue I now MOST of the time can correct me with a counterintuitive reflex. I look for the opposite of the reaction and this brings me back to a place of balance and "creative indifference". Previous discussion in the text about this is found in Working Alliance, Dialogue, Motivational Interviewing and Phenomenology.

115

The story goes that Buddha was visiting a temple with his cook who travelled with him. He was met and received with high reverence and taken to his chamber. The cook was shuffled off by the monks to the kitchen and told to prepare Buddha's meal.

"He will get it when I am fit and ready!" declared the cook.

The monks were upset and rushed to Buddha immediately to insist the throw the cook in jail or better still kill him for his insolence.

"No, you must not do that" said the Buddha.

"Why, not oh Buddha?" said the monks.

"Because he is my teacher," said the Buddha.

"No," said the monks disbelieving, "what can he teach you oh Buddha."

"Patience," said the Buddha.

Working Alliance and Management

The story of *Buddha's Cook* conjures the scene of the tranquil manager, serenely patience through lessons learnt practicing a paradoxical and dialogical approach to gestalt management. This is indeed a pleasant scene but of course such sunny days are only part of the "weather" of the work place – rain and storms are also sure to follow. There are times when the organisation as a whole may not be amenable to the time and effort required to achieve the more complex relational rewards of a field perspective. It requires that, work being work, that tasks be done! In such a case it is incumbent on the manager to be able to move things forward in some way. From a gestalt perspective this means not only of the guidance of phenomenological and dialogical principles of our approach, but also those of *experiment* which arise from the behavioural influence on gestalt therapy (Perls 1971, Kepner 1971, O'Neill and O'Neill 2008).

The principles of therapeutic alliance of are benefit as they offer interventions which are attuned to both relationship and task. In the first example where the staff member was about to resign, I realised afterwards it was my work with challenging clients had helped guide my intervention as a manager.

Freud described a working alliance in working with schizophrenia, (Inderbitzen, 1990). He noticed that in working with people experiencing schizophrenia that even in the midst of such chaotic disorder there exists in some corner of the mind a functional aspect of the person. The therapeutic TASK **is** to empathically seek out and delineate the non psychotic part of the ego, establish a meaningful communication and nurture its growth and expansion.

This offers us the beginning of a step-by-step set of guiding principles for working with ANY disordered system, be it individual, couple, family, group or community. In systems language we could say -

- emphatically seek out and delineate the functional part of the system,
- establish a meaningful communication and relationship
- and nurture is growth and expansion.

In the example above, I could delineate the functional and potentially dysfunctional behaviours of both the staff member and I as manager. I then formed an alliance around a "win-win" outcome for both. The Gestalt approach which came into play is the reflex to see this as a dialogical process. This means the manager must be willing to enter the situation and be present as a human being. This is to share a commitment allowing for a space developing between each person, which is authentic and human. This meaningful communication and relationship have a shared nature and are not a "doing to" by one to the other.

Rogers (1942) refined these principles in his theory and practice and while he is better remembered for his positive self regard, non-directive approach and empathy, he stressed an important balance which was that of congruence – being real, or in gestalt terms authentic.

At this point it may be useful to define these terms theoretically and provide an overview of how Gestalt therapy may contribute to management, and specifically the notion of being an "authentic" manager. Perls later refined and simplified his work he developed a model of the personality which has not been widely discussed in the gestalt literature (Perls 1969). He described the personality as like the many layers of an onion with the authentic self at the core and various layers around it caused by childhood pain and trauma so at the outer edge were the role-playing and cliché levels.

Peeling the Onion

The model below outlines various layers Perls suggested developed overtime. He described the layers of the personality from the "outside" in, like peeling an onion. This starts with the Cliché layer which is the level people learn to negotiate everyday life – "Hi, how's the weather?" Next is a more substantial experience of self which are the roles we have learnt or taken on. I define these as a habitual way of thinking feeling and acting – in essence a learnt reflex.

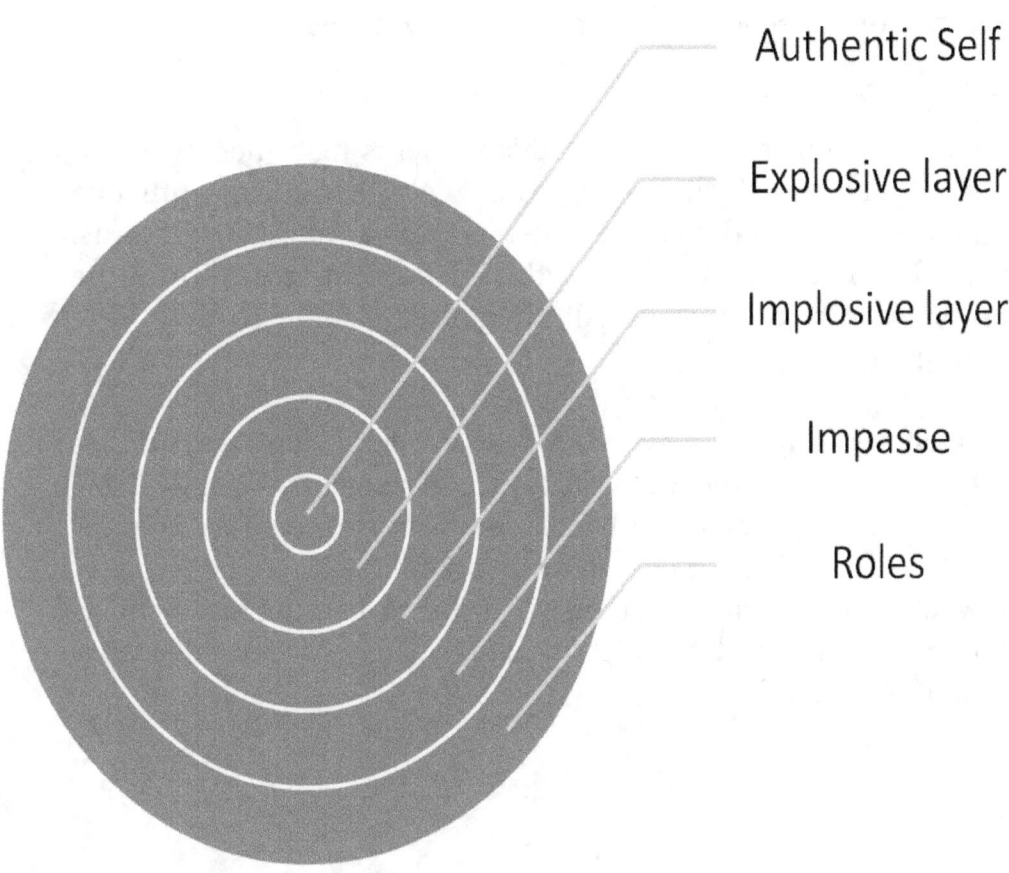

Authentic Self

Explosive layer

Implosive layer

Impasse

Roles

Perls noted in therapy that these were often the first contacts he met and that when he frustrated what he sensed where manipulative roles, other layers appeared. The first of these was the stuck point or impasse which was followed by an internalising layer he termed implosive. Therapeutically the trauma of explosive level emotions, which he classified as joy, orgasm, anger and grief, were modulated by self and other and existed underneath the implosive layer. He saw the direction for therapy to be inwards to the authentic self where the client could then become freed from outer roles which constrained the person.

One of the many critiques of this model is its rather fixed and static nature, which does not allow for immediate authentic behaviour but dooms the person to a struggle inwards. Traditionally we would teach this model and critique it in the first year of training gestalt therapists, mainly so they were aware of it.

Whatever critiques may exist of this model, including its rather fixed and distinctive ways of "layering" people, it does describe the experiences manager have in negotiating their role. To what extent is their relationship with others "role bound" and in what way or context may it be useful to be authentic, and is there a mixed reality which is paradoxically "both/and" rather than "either/or".

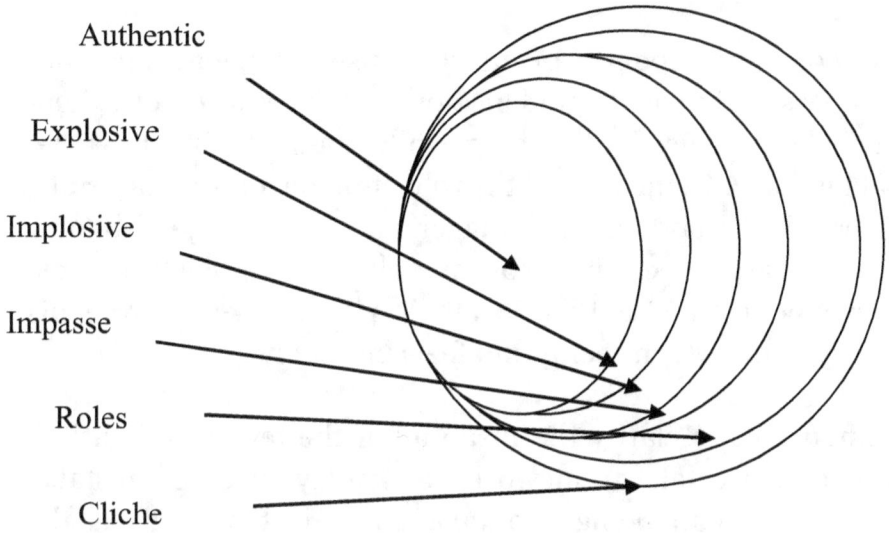

My own sense of this model early on was that its main fault, for whatever its uses, lay in the fixed nature and the determinism of placing authentic natures and behaviours within other experiences without direct spontaneous expression and access. I therefore altered the model slightly (above) to bring the authentic to the surface.

In this adapted model, a person approached in a certain way would thus be authentic, from a different angle mostly authentic but with a veneer of cliché or role while from a third angle would be primarily in a role without much connection at all to who they are in a spontaneous way. Even in saying this and altering the model, I am aware that we are using two dimensional models and rather fixed static language to describe a human being who is most assuredly more complex and rich than any model can hope to capture.

Authentic Self and Roles in Management

If this or any model can make sense of behaviour and experiences and provide guidance or principles to follow, then the model can be used, like a map, while not mistaking it for the actual territory. In the case of the role of manager, one can start to discriminate both as a manager and a "managed" if our behaviours are experienced by ourselves and each other as relatively honest and authentic, albeit with a veneer of role, or primarily a role which seems and feels inauthentic.

It is important to clarify the meaning of the term "authentic", within this Gestalt framework, as many people mistake authentic to mean being spontaneous or just saying exactly what we think and feel. This was evident in therapies in the 1960's and 1970's and even within Fritz Perls' famous "Gestalt prayer" which began "I do my thing and you do your thing".

Contemporary Gestalt therapy with its dialogical, relational base and attention to field theory does not go along with such an individualistic paradigm. Two of the most eminent trainers and writers in the field, Erving and Miriam Polster, state how spontaneity by itself is only half the requirement for authentic living. It reaches completion through relationship and responsiveness to the other (Polster and Polster, 1973). This is much like a dance duo who must thus attend to each others' spontaneity as well as their own in order to dance well. Hence we can define authenticity in shorthand as being responsively spontaneous.

When this is compared to behaviour which happens from a role, the difference becomes more obvious. A role in this sense then is a reflex or habit, and has little connection to the other in a responsive and spontaneous way. The simple formula for this is as follows –

A Role is a **Habit**ual way of
- o **Think**ing
- o **Feel**ing and
- o **Act**ing

On many occasions the role will happen outside of awareness, and it is this lack of awareness that often stimulates people to feel "role bound" or trapped. Some roles carry the cost of being a "learnt helplessness" as with the work by Martin Seligman. Seligman's original work with dogs was such that the dogs were in a cage with an electrified floor. They would be shocked and would try to escape but were unable to. After a time they stop trying to escape. They had learnt they were helpless. However once the cage was taken away and the dogs were shocked again they remain on the electrified floor. Even though the field conditions had changed they still operated from a learnt helplessness position. The researchers then dragged the dogs off the floor to show they could escape but when place back on the floor they still stayed there. They needed to be dragged off the floor nearly as many times as they had been shocked to learn they were no longer helpless. This research is a useful metaphor for clients, staff and managers alike as it reminds us that while some changes are immediate and spontaneous others need significant "unlearning". It takes time for an old role to decrease while a new role takes its place. Therefore there are behaviours which arise spontaneously in the person/environment and are experienced as "authentic". Other behaviours and relationships appear, as with the dogs, to be learnt behaviours or roles. It may of course be difficult at times to distinguish between the each however a guide is the authentic behaviour and relationship carries with more conscious awareness and choice, while the role may feel more automatic and restrictive at times.

Task Roles and Relational Roles

In management it would seem obvious that this "authentic self" as well as that of the "role" behaviours and relationships are both useful. At this point also it is useful to differentiate between an assigned role, which is a job and set of tasks someone is employed to do, compared to behaviour determined by habitual responses. This discrimination may be of use to managers, as often there is a sense that being a manager is opposite to being authentic, or needs boundaries which are rigidly defined. It is helpful therefore in any management situation to discriminate between aspects of the relationship in an organisation that is defined by the task (of which one has authority over another) and not confuse this with the relational aspects which are authentically fitting to each person and not prescribed by an organisation. Further, there may be times when the tasks of the organisation may be impacted by the confusion between these task roles and relational roles and the resultant needs for the individual to feel they need to act in role bound ways when they do not. Examples of this usually arise around issues of power and interpersonal relationships.

Transactional Analysis (TA) defines roles we play in order to manipulate to get our desired result. The classic triad of Parent, Adult and Child roles in TA were developed as the earliest relationship roles we develop and tend to arise easily in social situations and become enduring.

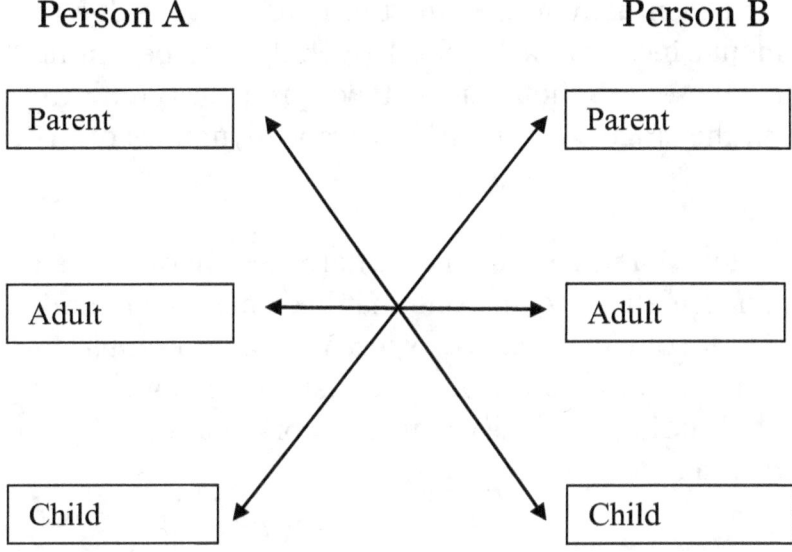

Person A   Person B

Parent   Parent

Adult   Adult

Child   Child

The role of manager seems immanently suitable within a TA frame work to become the Parent and in such a situation the complementary role of the "managed" is that of the Child. The desired alternative in TA, with awareness, is to choose an Adult to Adult relationship which is marked by assertiveness and relative equality **as a person**.

The manager who wants to achieve this Adult to Adult relationship may be stymied by the "managed" staff member who is caught in the role of Child no matter what the manager may say, purely and simply because of a reaction by the staff member to the **assigned** role, to which they **ascribe** Parent to the manager

In such a situation the manager for all intents and purposes may be pushed eventually to become the Parent, again due to the complementariness of each role. Hopefully it is becoming obvious that these are not linear type processes but are systemic or in the language of Gestalt therapy, dynamics of the field.

The table below summarises the differences between an authentic management style and one that becomes role bound. These are not, of course, *separate* experiences as presented in the table, but on a continuum which we may move along, back and forth, depending on the context, work culture, staff member and issue.

	Authentic Manager	**Role Bound**
Organisational Role	Assigned	Ascribed
Complementary Role	Manager/staff	Parent/Child
Power Issues	Task	Relationship
Relationship	Authentic/Assertive	Manipulative
Management Style	Collaborative	Authoritarian/rigid

It is common for managers to assume and carry out their assigned power through a working relationship as manager and staff. In such situations the tasks get done in a collaborative way while showing leadership and with resultant authentic and assertive relationships in the work culture. When a manager becomes role bound, and this may be due to the organisation or work culture and not just the manager, then Parent Child relationships appear (or already existed). In such circumstances there are power issues expressed in the relationship which become manipulative and eventually the manager feels forced into a rigid authoritarian position.

Such "role lock" behaviours are common in organisations and to undo this needs a climate accepted by all parties which consciously is aware of these processes. Instead of manipulating staff and manager strives to achieve authentic and assertive relationships within the assigned roles of manager and managed. This needs continual dialogue and vigilance, as well as training and awareness-raising, so the work culture is maintained in a way that allows task roles to work to their full ability, supported by people who authentically occupy those positions.

When we can place people first and then support them to engage with the assigned task roles of their organisation, we can achieve a workplace which is both psychologically and emotionally healthy, while productive and task focused. The gestalt approach provides a set of principles and a philosophy which complements work as a manager. This is in areas of human relationships as well as with the tasks wanted of and between one another in the workplace. This approach to management has been of particular value in helping me move from the more individualistic "head space" of strategy and key performance indicators to that of a relational field. Here dialogical presence and the ethics of being authentic offer me and, hopefully others, a greater freedom in experimenting with new tasks and roles which make space for the personhood of each individual, be they manager or staff member alike.

Gestalt therapy provides support and direction to managers to work in an authentic way, in tune with modern management theories of complexity theory. The philosophies and practices within the Gestalt approach offer a bridge to include classical, neo-classical and modern theories of management. This is so when management theory struggles to come to terms with the paradoxical nature of issues such as control, humane concern, systems interactions, emergent change and working with organisational culture.

This book is a beginning in bridging these fields and for managers who may also be interested in Gestalt therapy. Gestalt organisational consultants do indeed offer much of benefit to the areas they work and I hope this text has encouraged managers to read further in the Gestalt Organisational literature. I also hope it offers the opportunity for further development and connection between each field.

Resource Articles

The Gestalt Field Perspective: Field Theoretical Strategy

Seán Gaffney and Brian O'Neill

> There are wholes, the behavior of which is not determined by
> that of their individual elements, but where the part – processes are
> themselves determined by the intrinsic nature of the whole.
> (Wertheimer, 1925 in Ellis 1938, p. 2)

This chapter provides operational definitions of the main field theories in gestalt therapy and their commonalities. It relates these conceptualizations of field theory to therapy, with a view to describing how one might apply the philosophy and principles of field theory in practice as a field perspective methodology. It also provides case material, comparing and contrasting the two main field approaches in gestalt therapy. Finally, it presents a heuristic list of principles guiding a strategy in practice common to all field theory approaches and suitable for application in gestalt therapy and research.

There are numerous influences on gestalt therapy, of which field theory is one. It is a core philosophical underpinning; yet, the construct of field theory has not been well understood, discussed, or applied to practice (Yontef 1993, Staemmler 2006, O'Neill 2008). Nor has it been well discriminated from a similar concept, that of systems theory, and this has lead to further confusion in both the construct and application of field theory in particular and gestalt therapy in general. (Latner 1983, Gaffney 2008).

Gestalt therapy assimilates the ideas of modern physics. Observations influence the nature and identity of the observed, not only metaphorically or phenomenologically, but also ontologically (O'Neill, 2008). Further, the connectedness and paradoxical nature of reality described by the organism-environment field (Perls, Hefferline and Goodman 1951) and the relativistic quantum field of physics are clearly consilient – more so than with therapies built on reductionist models of human behaviour that see simple causative effects in objects of therapy, similar to the ways Newton's Laws predicted outcomes.

This correlation of gestalt therapy with the field theory of modern physics allows therapists to move beyond the individual, reductionist nature of most of psychology. Psychotherapy based on such limited models sees the therapist and client as two distinct entities. Field theory supports gestalt therapists in taking the step of being aware of the "self" of the therapist – client, the "self" of the couple, of the group and the community. Such a perspective allows one to see patterns of these larger wholes at work, patterns of homeostasis, polarisation and growth as well as contact boundary dynamics (Gaffney, 2006), choosing to apply the life space of Lewin, the cycle of experience (Cleveland), the contact sequence (Perls, Hefferline, R., and Goodman) or the contact episode (Polsters) as a way to map the harmonic patterns underlying the apparent chaos of these aggregates.

In particular we are proposing a converging view of field theory in gestalt therapy, which we call a *field perspective,* to encompass the varieties of theory. This is partly in order to honor and respect our gestalt colleagues who find either Lewinian or Perls, Hefferline and Goodman approaches to field theory attractive, and partly to recognize that such a unified perspective expresses the holistic paradigm that gestalt practitioners – in name and nature – espouse. For one of us (Seán) my heart is still with the Lewinian field perspective – or, more honestly, the extrapolation of Lewin. For the other (Brian), I have an affinity with the field perspective of Perls, Hefferline and Goodman and Smuts.

It is the synthesis of these previously competing approaches that we shall now attempt, for both are present. To do this we begin with a therapist's description of Lewin's field theory and principles of application, and then move to how these inform practice in the case study that follows. We will subsequently consider this work theoretically and practically from a Perls, Hefferline and Goodman perspective, comparing and contrasting each. The convergence of these theories into ways of working will then be addressed, with the result of a common language and competencies for use in training, practice and research.

From Theory to Practice – A Lewinian Approach

Kurt Lewin pioneered the application of field thinking in physics to early work in experimental psychology as well as his highly influential contributions to the development of social psychology and group dynamics (Marrow 1969). His delineation of field theory eventually became a methodology embedded in a meta-theory (Gold, 1990). Lewin's thinking supports the notion that *field* is both ontologically real and present at the same time that it can be in part phenomenologically experienced. He distinguished this latter as the *life space*, though he used the terms *field* and *life space* synonymously (Staemmler 2006).

Lewin is the author of the formula B = f (P, E). In plain English: behavior is a function of the person in an environment. He gave the example of how the same ontological environment will be perceived in distinctly unique ways by a variety of persons, depending upon their roles, circumstances and needs. An example is as follows: A farmer might see a clump of rocks and thick bushes in the middle of a piece of fertile land as an obstruction to be removed in the interests of increased acreage and easier harvesting; a soldier might see it as a place of ambush or hiding; two rambling lovers might see it as an opportunity for private moments. As such, each life space carries its own distinct set of characteristics as a sub-set of whatever totality may exist.

Should any of the persons in the example change roles and circumstances, their experience of the clump would also change. If the soldier became a farmer, that in which he once hid and found safety would become either an obstruction to remove, or a reminder to cherish. Paraphrasing Lewin's thinking, the need organizes the life space. What we see as our environment and how we see and respond to it are related to our needs. Naturally, when the environment is not a clump of rocks and bushes, but rather other people, then needs meet needs, responses evoke responses and all the unpredictability of being in and of the world comes into dynamic play. This is also where life space and field can become difficult to separate; yet, we argue for the value, both theoretically and practically, in gestalt therapists making that separation. For the sake of clarity, what follows is a highly simplified and minimalist description of Lewinian field theory. The practical extrapolations from this simplification will follow in a mini-case illustration.

First, the person *has* a life space at the same time as the person is *of* the person/environment field. This will become clearer and its relevance more obvious as we proceed. The person will have a sense of being able to observe and describe the environment – and this sense of observability and describeability, and its content, *is* her life space. Since we cannot observe that of which we are ourselves a part, the person is unable to describe the field of which she is a part. She can however describe her experience of being influenced – and as soon as she distinguishes what or who is influencing her, she is taking a life space perspective. The life space is the environment as perceived by a person relating to it, usually depicted as a Jordan curve. Some of Lewin's doctoral candidates liked to call these "bathtubs" (Patnoe, 1988).

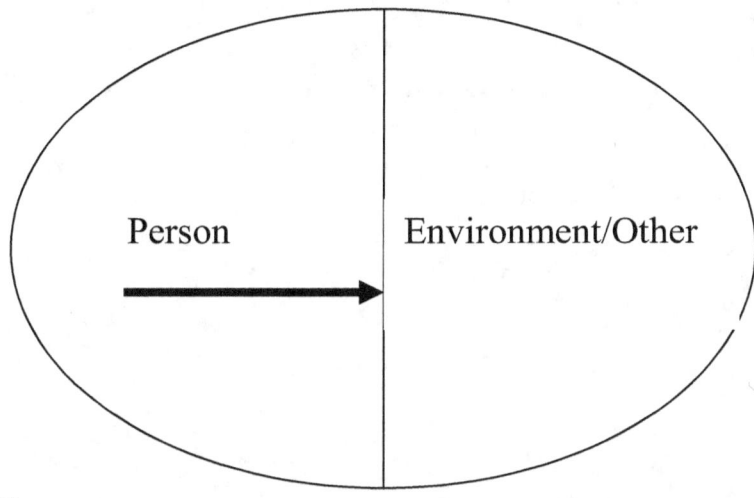

Figure 1

While the environmental other/others constitute the life space of the person, the wholeness of the person and her environment is the field of the person/environment, where each element is dynamically contributing to the self-organizing in the moment

135

and thus also over time. In this way, a person may experience quite a different sense of agency in respect to her life space than in respect to the field of which she is a contributing force.

This point becomes clearer when the environment of the life space is another person and viewed from that other's perspective simultaneously:

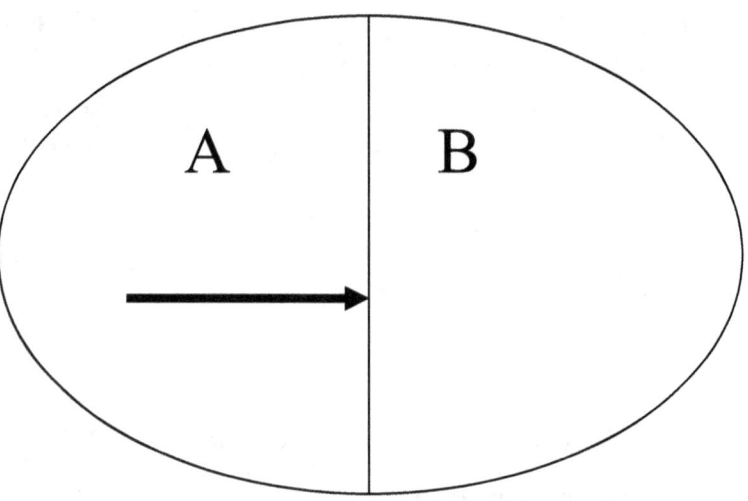

Figure 2

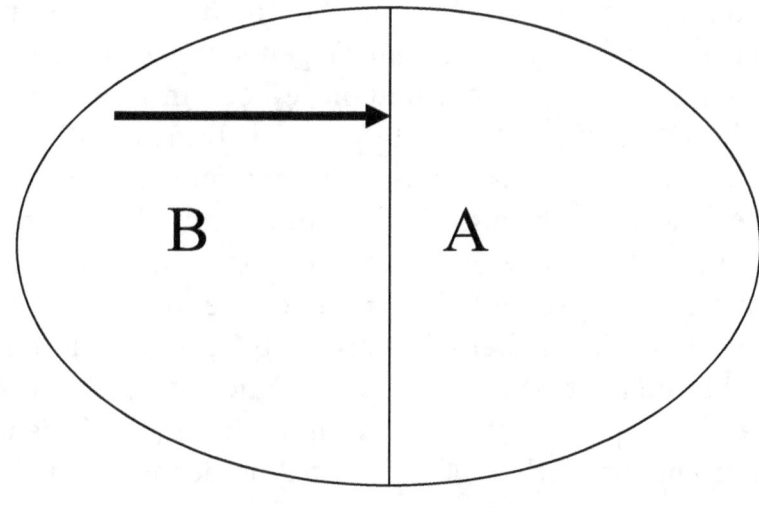

Figure 3

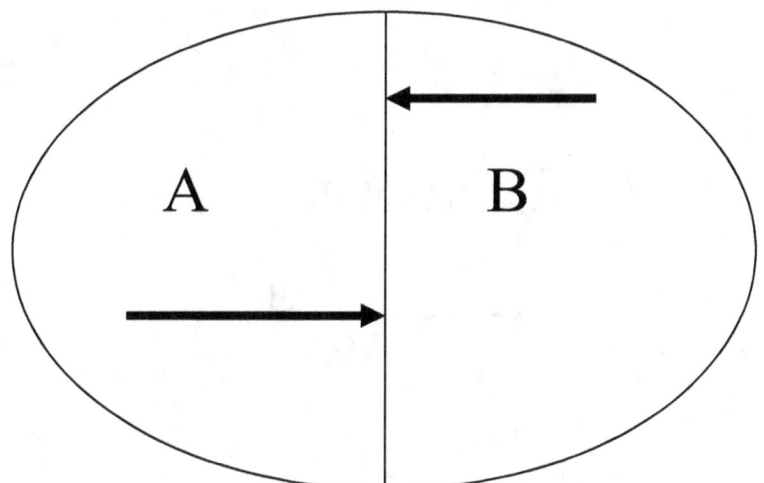

Figure 4

Here, the life space of A is A in relation to B (Figure 2). Simultaneously, the life space of B is B in relation to A (Figure 3). Merged and inextricably linked, they constitute the field of AB (Figure 4), to which may be added other environmental factors, bringing with them the totality of coexisting facts conceived of as mutually interdependent (Lewin, 1951), and of which only one of them may have been in awareness prior to their interaction. Concretely, each brings with it a past experience expressed in the present and aspirations for the future chosen through behaviours. Assuming that A is the client, the presence of the therapist now adds both a new life space for A as well as a life space for the therapist. At the same time, A is bringing her life space to therapy, so that it is possible to extrapolate that the life space of the therapist is both A and the life space of A, including B as representing the environmental other/others that A is dealing with in her life and which may well be the theme of the therapy:

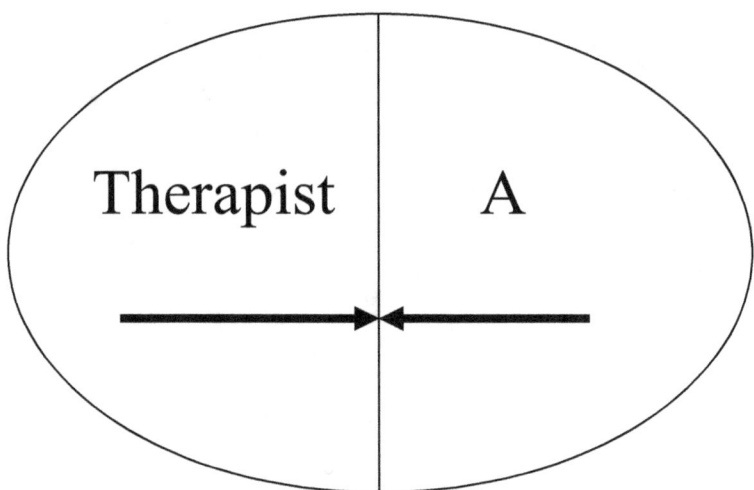

Figure 5.

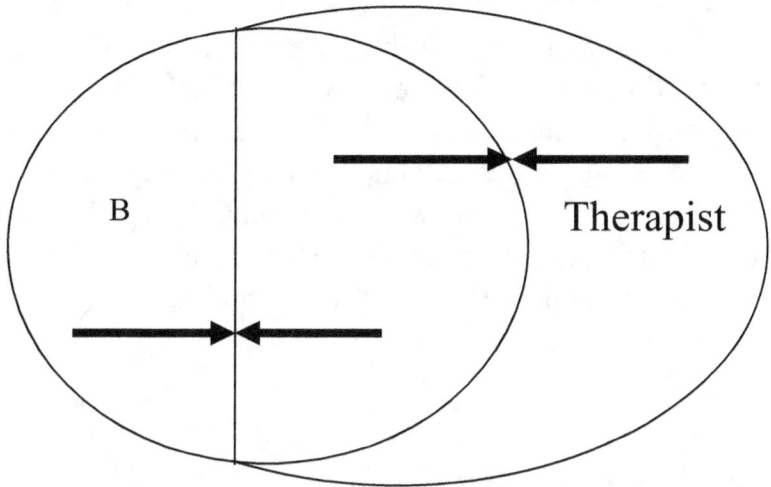

Figure 6

The therapist is meeting a client and the world of that client as she experiences it. Together, the combined life spaces dynamically constitute the therapist/client field, where each is both influencing and being influenced by all the other forces of that field. It is precisely this aspect of the therapeutic work that allows new and often surprising themes to emerge at the therapist-client contact boundary.

This is a good place to add an essential aspect of the perspective being presented here: the slash (/) or even hyphen (-) in the construct organism/-environment, usually taken to denote the contact boundary in gestalt therapy theory, is functionally identical to the line in the Jordan curve which is used to distinguish the person from the environment in Lewin's original work. So the Jordan curve highlights the person-contact boundary-environment dynamics of organism/-environment, though more explicitly from a psychological perspective (Staemmler 2006).

As a gestalt therapist, there is no investment in changing the client's behavior per se, but there is interest in exploring her perception of her life space, fully trusting that any change in her perception will emerge as changes to her life space and, therefore, allow her to make choices about her behavior which she may not have felt were previously possible. The agency is the client's, as are the choices and the actions. The therapeutic process is the possible catalyst for change.

An Illustrative Mini – Case

Anne is a new client, who comes to me on the recommendation of a close friend and gestalt trainee who knows of me through the training institute. Anne is a successful professional in her forties and moves quickly to her issue, the reason for coming to therapy. She has great difficulties in finding a long-term relationship, though no shortage of possible candidates: currently these are Bernard, Charlie and David. Bernard is her former husband. Charlie is her current lover. David is a former lover now back in her social sphere after a short absence immediately following their mutually agreed parting.

It soon transpires that Anne is currently meeting all three of them, though only having regular sexual relations with Charlie. She has had a night or so for old time's sake with David, and still feels attracted to Bernard. She feels that she really needs to make "a final choice" among them and settle down in a good relationship with a long-term commitment.

I become aware as I listen to Anne that there is a disparity that attracts my attention. As she talks of any one of the three, he becomes figural for me as the other two recede into the background. For Anne, mention of any one of them instantly raises the other two as equally energized figures. In life space terms, her environment is not Bernard and/or Charlie and/or David. It seems to me more like BernardCharlieDavid, a trio as a unit.

This becomes explicit any time I attempt to raise her awareness around her feelings for each of the three – the other two come instantaneously into the work. So I take this as it is, see the trio as her environmental other, and begin working more consistently with Anne's experience of all three as a unit. So I ask her to describe the synthesis of characteristics – both attractive to her and unattractive – that they, taken together, embody. It is in this work that Anne herself begins differentiating between them. For example, she will name what is for her an attractive characteristic embodied in the trio, and then begin reflecting aloud on which of them has "most" of it, and "less" and "least".

At the same time, whenever one of the three seems to be emerging most clearly, she will immediately correct herself for having omitted each of the other two, and bring them into a newly energized three-in-one or even one-in-three.

As Anne and I move further into this work, I become increasingly aware of another figure forming between us. As the son of an alcoholic father who was often angry and occasionally violent, I have a built – in early warning system for the presence of anger or ill intent towards me. I see this as a form of mild paranoia, generally useful and occasionally more projective than I am aware of in the moment. Anne had a way of glancing sideways at me, and that set off the alarm bells of my early warning system. Having reflected between sessions in an attempt to raise my awareness around how much of this was mine as opposed to hers I decided to raise it with her the next time it happened. So, she glanced sideways at me, I reacted as before, and I shared my experience with her, asking if she were in any way angry with me. Anne reassured me that she was not in any way the slightest bit angry with me – until I had suggested that she might have been! I asked her if she could accept that I drew her attention to any occasion when I felt myself resonating to possible anger, and she agreed. This now became part of our interactions as the therapy continued.

There were then two major themes present in our work, one of which Anne had brought with her as an element of her existing life space, (her felt need to decide between three men and her difficulty in doing so) and the other (my bodily response to a particular glance of hers) I brought as a feature of my life space. At the same time, since it did not belong to a relationship with her prior to the therapy, it was clearly of the field of Me-Anne-Anne's life space. My reflections here were exploring my possible anger towards Anne, or even towards any or all of the three men in her life. While I certainly liked her, I did not trace any feelings of emotional or physical attraction strong enough to evoke my jealousy and resentment. And so the work continued.

Session twelve marked a turning point in our work and probably in Anne's life. She was yet again extolling the virtues of all three men, and becoming self – critical at her inability to decide among them, when I had a sudden image of a pair of gloves. I bracketed this apparently inappropriate image and turned my full attention back to Anne. The image returned, and as I hesitated to deal with it, came at me in a highly energized form, visually and verbally. When Anne came to a pause in her narrative, I asked her if I could share a curious experience I was having as I sat there with her. She agreed. So I told her of how I had had a clear visual image of gloves as well as the thought "gloves" as I listened to her. She looked me straight in my eyes, sat back in her chair and I saw her eyes water. She sighed, and started crying. Talking through her tears, she told how, as a child, her parents had insisted on her wearing woolen mittens as soon as the weather turned cold. They were itchy and made her feel clumsy as she could not fully use her fingers.

When it rained, they became sodden and cold. Sometimes they would be covered in ice and feel heavy and uncomfortable. She had tried "losing" them, only to be given a new pair almost immediately. After she had left home and started traveling, she found herself beginning to collect fine gloves, usually of soft leather, and always a perfect fit. She now had a special drawer at home for her collection, and would occasionally sort through them – though never wear any of them outdoors.

As she continued to muse on this theme, she began reflecting on her life and how she generally disliked doing anything she felt that she was "supposed" to do. She could see that she sometimes stayed in an uncomfortable situation longer than she needed, and had difficulties making her own choices and acting on them.The session drew to a close as the image which had emerged became transformed – and was still transforming – into a metaphor that had meaning for Anne in her life. This now became the theme for the following sessions, and BernardCharlieDavid receded into the background, with very few references to them other than in the context of this new theme. Anne's life space had changed as an energized figure had emerged from the field of possibilities.

Within three months, Anne had unexpectedly met a teenage love, Eric, reconnected with him, and they had become lovers. Within a further three months, they had set up house together and married. Anne continued in therapy with me for a short while after their marriage and we eventually agreed to close our work together.

During this period, I had occasionally reflected on the other theme – that of anger, and the possible connections between Anne, her parents and me. The sideways glance still made occasional appearances. I decided that this was now of the field and that if it had any figural energy for Anne, then she could choose to raise it with me. She never did.

From Practice to Theory – Some Reflections

We mentioned earlier that the work is not focused on changing a client's behavior. It is focused on exploring the client's life space from different perspectives and allowing new behaviors to emerge from any changed perception that may occur. Thus, the therapist did not influence Anne in reaching a *new* perspective. Rather, the environment consisted of BernardCharlieDavid and attempts at distinguishing among them, and that, in turn, led to a more fundamental theme in Anne's life.

The therapist's introduction of anger, emerging as it did from the past he brought with him as part of the ground of his life space and resonating in the here-and-now with Anne was an energized figure for him, but not for Anne.

The image of the gloves, and its transformation into a metaphor, is clearly of the therapist/Anne field. This image emerged in the therapist and connected directly to a significant event in Anne's childhood. Lewin's thinking includes the notion of vectors – energies or forces that have an origin, a magnitude and a direction. The gloves image had its origin in Anne's childhood experience, and her strong memories of that experience, including their antecedent in the glove collection, but the metaphorical meaning developed for her as she saw her life through the lens of that metaphor. At the same time, the image had its origin in the therapist with sufficient magnitude to remain figural for him and with a clear direction – Anne.

The process whereby an event of Anne's past emerged as an image in the therapist and returned to Anne is the magic and the mystery of a field approach. Therapist and client are of a field of their life history, their present – both separately and together – and are influenced by the self-organizing dynamics of which they are also influential parts.

There is no doubt that the process of the gloves image can be, or soon will be, open to a generally acceptable "scientific" explanation. Our interest is not in such an explanation as we are more concerned here with the experience of this process and its value in a therapeutic setting. By working from a Lewinian field approach a gestalt therapist can move from the pragmatics of a life space perspective to the usage relevant to a recipient or channel of energy in the field of which the therapist is a co-creating part and back to the life spaces involved.

The Field of Perls, Hefferline and Goodman

Gestalt therapy has offered a rather distinctive paradigm from which to view the person and reality. While later theorists such as Yontef, Parlett and Wheeler have cited field theory (particularly that of Kurt Lewin) as a key pillar or philosophical underpinning to gestalt therapy, it is the original text of Perls, Hefferline and Goodman (1951) that offers a very startling, vibrant and easily missed description of it.

From the beginning of the theoretical half of the book, they outline a view of the self as intrinsically part of an overall organism – environment field. In a manner reminiscent of mystical writing, the self is seen as indistinguishable and a priori, *at one* with the all that is, and not only in an epistemological sense, but also ontologically:

> *Let us call this interacting of organism and environment in any function the "organism – environment field;" and let us remember no matter how we theorize about impulses, drives etc., it is always to such an interacting field that we are referring, and not to an isolated animal. Where the organism is mobile in a great field and has a complicated internal structure, like an animal, it seems plausible to speak of it by itself – as, for instance, the skin and what is contained in it – but this is simply an illusion due to the fact that the motion through space and the internal detail call attention to themselves against the relative stability and simplicity of the background. (Perls, Hefferline and Goodman 1951, 228)*

It would be easy to skip over this conceptualization or become lost in the language. However the implication of what is being said is stark.

Our sense of a separate self is an illusion.

146

The experience of separateness in sensing the self is illusory, or at best built upon the functioning of a separate ego-sense of self that develops later in early life. As the child starts to discriminate *self* and *not self,* such ego functions arise, and as the child learns to represent reality symbolically, this languaging of self and ego becomes the personality. It is how we describe ourselves in words and concepts.

One of the two definitions of the self found in Perls, Hefferline and Goodman, that *self is a system of contacts in the organism – environment field*, provides the scope to move beyond the separate ego – sense of self to the potential in many selves that come into being and then fade back into the ground. Hence, when two or more people become systematized in their contact with each other, they are a *self.*

Perls, Hefferline and Goodman Field Theory in Principle and Practice

The text of *Gestalt Therapy: Excitement and Growth in the Human Personality* (Perls, Herfferline, and Goodman, 1951) is in essence two books – a book of theory and a book of practice. At first glance, it appears to the reader that the practice section flows from the theory section and explicates a "means whereby" the theory can be applied in life and therapy. However, on closer inspection, this assumption is partially incorrect; the experiments in the (original) second book are not as closely related to the theory as one might hope. This appraisal is based on the understanding that a clear approach to practice for field theory at the time the book was written was lacking; indeed, the majority of experiments are directed towards work with individuals in the reductionist fashion characteristic of therapy at that time, (and even the group and couples applications of field theory were as yet in fledging stages). We will now delineate the key field theory principles embedded in the book of theory in Perls, Hefferline and Goodman which guide our work as therapists from a field perspective.

Principle One: The Whole Determines the Parts
The core principle of a field perspective "...lies in the insight that the whole determines the parts" (Perls, Hefferleine and Goodman, 1951, xi). This encourages gestalt therapists to escape the reductionist nature in some corners of clinical psychology that sees only the individual of the therapist and the separate client. To move beyond this point is to develop an awareness of the "self" of the therapist-client dyad and of the reality of nonindependence. This extends to the "self" of the couple, of the "self" of the group and of the community. Such a perspective supports gestalt therapists in seeing patterns of these larger wholes at work, patterns of homeostasis, polarisation and growth.

Principle Two: Contact Boundaries
The self is a system of contacts in the organism-environment field. The person is not contemplated as a separate individual but always as an organism – environment field. The organism contacts the environment at a boundary and takes in what it needs, keeping out what it does not need, and this is contact. It is contact which denotes identity (or form), yet this identity is one in which the basic elements are constantly taking form and dissolving

Principle Three: Homeostasis and Growth
The organism has two main needs – balance and growth – and organises the field to meet these needs, e.g. if I'm hungry, I organise the field into food/not food. Over time the contact the

organism has with its environment forms patterns, repetitions, habits and creative adjustments to novel stimuli that form a residue of experience. These are the patterns of contact, frequently laid down in procedural memory, that become maintained over time and constitute that portion of the "self" known by gestalt therapists as personality function. This is a different view of the self than models of personality in which the self is a fixed entity "within." In gestalt therapy the abiding patterns of personality function to orient the constantly forming experience of self.

Principle Four: Wisdom of the Organism
Figure /ground formation, when allowed to operate unobstructed, attends to the immediate needs of the organism. People usually come to therapy with this process diminished and blunted in some way through fixed gestalten and redundant creative adjustments.

Principle Five: Paradoxical Agency
Gestalt therapists study the operation of the contact boundary in the organism-environment field. As stated before, gestalt therapy works with wholes. Early, non-field oriented practitioners talked about gestalt therapy and the need for the therapist to "exercise control" of the therapeutic situation, which was often defined as "the therapist being able to persuade or coerce the patient into following the procedures he has set" (Fagan and Shepherd, 1970, pp. 91 – 92).

More current theorists, like Hycner (1993), have described this as a paradoxical process of searching for balance between choice and acceptance. This is described in the original text of Perls, Hefferline and Goodman as the "middle mode" of being the space in between active and passive functioning, where the person is accepting, attending and growing into the solution, and with the substitution of readiness (or faith) in the current situation for the security of apparent control (Perls, Hefferline and Goodman, 1951; 1984 edition). We call this paradoxical agency.

Integration and Application in Gestalt Therapy

A contemporary field perspective in gestalt therapy can be established by denoting core commonalities between Lewinian and Perls, Hefferline and Goodman conceptualizations of the field and through identifying strategies available to gestalt therapists in working with field dynamics.Whereas the Perls, Hefferline and Goodman understanding of field dynamics requires critical realism (the ontological commitment that permits some kind of unseen, but real field to exist, similar to the wireless fields that allow computers to pick up the internet simply by being present within the spheres of their influence), the Lewinian perspective requires an epistemological consideration, because it focuses on *the method* by which the life space of the client in his or her environment comes to know and be known in the life space of the therapist.

We shall now return to the case study presented previously, following the therapist's process and noting how each field perspective is of use at certain points, not only as an attitude, but more specifically and importantly as a guiding principle that in tight therapeutic sequences directs and enables gestalt therapy.

A Comparison of Field Theory Approaches in Practice

I become aware as I listen to Anne that there is a disparity which attracts my attention. As she talks of any one of the

150

three, he becomes figural for me as the other two recede into the background. For Anne, mention of any one of them instantly raises the other two as equally energized figures. In life space terms, her environment is not Bernard and/or Charlie and/or David. It seems to me more like BernardCharlieDavid, a trio as a unit. (Therapist, from case study)

The therapist is aware of patterns of the field of Anne-and-therapist and the difference between the two. A traditional counselor in psychoanalysis, CBT or Rogerian/Egan counselling would probably not think to be aware of this. The awareness of patterns in figure-ground formation operates within a field perspective and uses terms of "figural," "background," "energized figures," and "life space." These patterns of client-and-therapist are developed around clear experience – what the client is saying and how this is received by the therapist.

This becomes explicit any time I attempt to raise her awareness around her feelings for each of the three – the other two come instantaneously into the work. So I take this as it is, see the trio as her environmental other, and begin working more consistently with Anne's experience of all three as a unit. So I ask her to describe the synthesis of characteristics – both attractive to her and unattractive – which they, taken together, embody. (Therapist, from case study)

Now there is an experiment which is directed by the field perspective of Lewin's approach – describing the three as one unit, as an "environment." This is less likely from a Perls, Hefferline and Goodman approach to field where the term used might be "confluence of figures" rather than noting the three as a figural "environment." Neither of these requires an actual field to be in operation as the reaction by the therapist is based on patterns noted in explicit reality "as it is."

As Anne and I move further into this work, I become increasingly aware of another figure forming between us. As the son of an alcoholic father who was often angry and occasionally violent, I have a built-in early warning system for the presence of anger or ill intent towards me. I see this as a form of mild paranoia, generally useful and occasionally more projective than I am aware of in the moment. Anne had a way of glancing sideways at me which set off the alarm bells of my early warning system. (Therapist, from case study)

From a field perspective anything figural is worthy of attention, either for client or therapist as they are both in connection to each other and nothing unconnected ever happens. The challenge for the field perspective therapist is to make sense of this and know what to do with it, if anything at all. Both Lewin and Perls, Hefferline and Goodman approaches would allow the value of this awareness and attention to any vibrant figure in the field, simply because it is there.

Having reflected between sessions in an attempt to raise my awareness around how much of this was more mine than hers, I decided to raise it with her the next time it happened. So she glanced sideways at me, I reacted as before – and I shared my experience with her and asked if she was in any way angry with me. Anne reassured me that she was not in any way the slightest bit angry with me – until I had suggested that she might have been! I asked her if she could accept that I drew her attention to any occasion when I felt myself resonating to possible anger, and she agreed. This now became part of our interactions as the therapy continued. (Therapist, from case study)

Here we witness a clearly intentional action on the part of the therapist, a dialogical movement to share the presence of the therapist with an awareness that this is a field experiment about the "resonance" to the client in the field, with the client as environment to the therapist's person. The term resonance is what sets this aside from the theories of traditional practice that use descriptions of connections between client and therapist of reflection, empathy, and transference, etc. – processes that happen *as if* in a vacuum. The term "resonance" indicates a defined physical process of connection, as with wave theory in physics. This action could be equally explained by either Lewin or Perls, Hefferline and Goodman approaches.

Session 12 marked a turning-point in our work and probably in Anne's life. She was yet again extolling the virtues of all three men, and becoming self-critical at her inability to decide between them, when I had a sudden image of a pair of gloves. I bracketed this apparently inappropriate image and turned my full attention back to Anne. The image returned, and as I hesitated to deal with it, came at me in a highly energized form, visually and verbally. When Anne came to a pause in her narrative, I asked her if I could share a curious experience I was having as I sat there with her. She agreed. So I told her of how I had had a clear visual image of gloves as well as the thought "gloves" as I listened to her. She looked me straight in my eyes, sat back in her chair and I saw her eyes water. She sighed, and started crying. Talking through her tears, she told how, as a child, her parents had insisted on her wearing woollen mittens as soon as the weather turned cold. They were itchy and made her feel clumsy as she could not fully use her fingers. When it rained, they became sodden and cold. Sometimes they would be covered in ice and feel heavy and uncomfortable. She had tried "losing" them, only to be given a new pair almost immediately. After she had left home and started traveling, she found herself beginning to collect fine gloves, usually of soft leather, and always a perfect fit. She now had a special drawer at home for her collection, and would occasionally sort through them – though never wear any of them outdoors. (Therapist from case study)

This session develops a very particular aspect of the field perspective which goes clearly beyond the bounds of traditional reductionist paradigms of therapy. The insistent figure of the gloves appears at first to have no connection to either the therapist or the client, and seems unexplainable. Unless there is other information not being provided, then this stands out as an event which does not make sense within a non-field theory perspective. A Lewinian approach allows for the equivalence or relevance for each figure that arises as potentially in the field and the inter-relationship. Certainly, expecting or experimenting with something that seems *only* relevant to the therapist would be advocated by both field approaches. We would argue that only a field approach that allows for a figure which is clearly within the field of the therapist-client and has no apparent relevance would be expected nonetheless of having potentially significant relevance for the client. It could also be argued that this speaks of implicit forces at work and at this point we may find a "parting of the ways" for Lewinian and Perls, Hefferline and Goodman approaches. There is a discrimination point between these theories or approaches at which the figure of the glove either developed from the sustained ongoing interaction between client and therapist (and hence belonged to the life space of each together), or the

154

therapist was somehow in "wireless" mode and actually responding to a connection between the client and therapist from a real, albeit invisible connection of the type described by Sheldrake, in biology, and Bohm, in physics (O'Neill 2008). For the wireless mode to operate, an ontological field is assumed whatever its nature may be.

From a purist Lewinian perspective, the mention of the gloves would be less likely to be made a prominent principle for guiding practice; still, it could be incorporated or explained through allowing for the equal relevance of all figures in a field and was *somehow* figural for the therapist by a process of meeting between client and therapist.

From a Perls, Hefferline and Goodman perspective the beliefs that there are no isolated events and that there exists a "self" of therapist-client allows the gloves more fully to be a figure of this self. However, while the Perls, Hefferline and Goodman contribution to the field perspective explains these selves in operation as a unified whole and stresses that this is "...the original, undistorted, natural approach to life" (Perls, Hefferline and Goodman, 1984 edition, p. viii), it does not explain the separate experiences of reality that each individual has, nor how something like the glove event could happen at the contact boundary. While it advocates an ontological position akin to critical realism, it does not have the explanatory power to connect the notion of self to the field as a whole, the same way that Maxwell in physics defined the electromagnetic field.

While theorists diverge in the need for an actual field to exist, in practice there is less importance placed on such theoretical nuances, which are left to academic writing, and more attention is given by therapists to the principles that guide practice and the attitudes and skills they can use to support themselves while engaged in psychotherapy.

We are in agreement with Malcolm Parlett, who calls for a theory of practice when he writes:

More attention to our theories of practice would help bring about a rapprochement between our practical methodology and the theoretical descriptions and justifications we have in our literature. They would avoid the impression growing that discussions about theoretical differences are played out in one space, while what people actually do is consigned to another space altogether. (Parlett 2008 unpublished manuscript)

A Theory of Practice in a Field Perspective

The following section outlines interlocking theoretical precepts or principles, informing strategies that therapists might employ and that delineate the attitudes and practices utilized in a field perspective.

Principle One: The Whole Determines the Parts
Nothing unconnected ever happens. Theoretically this is seen by many as the *essence* of the field (Parlett, 1991) and is clearly evident in the original text by Perls, Hefferline and Goodman. This idea also influenced theorists such as Smuts, Wertheimer and Lewin. From this holistic perspective individual *phenomena are determined by the whole field* and client progress and outcome are functions of the whole field, not just dependent on isolated causal factors such as client motivation, the skill of the therapist, or targeted techniques and interventions.

Working from the whole, a therapist pays attention to the environment, history, and culture. A therapist remains open to "the web of relationship" (Yontef 1993) and anything of "possible relevance" (Parlett 1997), potentialities in the mix that at first may not appear connected, and encourages a willingness to shift viewpoints and consider phenomena from many perspectives, knowing that nothing unconnected ever happens. He or she may just not as yet see the connections. This attunes the gestalt therapist to also consider nothing as random but to be linked in some way to something else in an order that is mostly implicit but can become explicit through awareness, dialogue and experiment.

Principle Two: Consider Self to Be Process

The self was originally defined as the system of contacts in an organism – environment field (Perls, Hefferline and Goodman) and described by Lewin's equation, $B = f(P, E)$ to depict a person's state as corresponding to the behavior and the situation (Lewin, 1952, p. 242). This contextualizes the experience of self.

Like a clear figure that emerges from the ground, the organism is always part of a field and is defined by that field. Furthermore, fields are always in flux. In a sense, everything is always in the process of passing away. Thus, a therapist remains open to change and is reluctant to accept any fixedness about persons or situations. This stance attunes the gestalt therapist to look for shifts in process and "evidence of difference" and to turn more fixed categorizations into language representing processes. For instance, a therapist might turn "I have depression" into "I am experiencing depressing of feelings."

Principle Three: Follow the Organization of the Field

Needs and interest organize the field (and more so the lifespace). The person has two main needs, balance and growth (Perls, Hefferline, and Goodman, 1951), and may have multiple interests and curiosities. The person organises the field to meet these needs, to pursue interest, and to satisfy curiosity. How one makes sense of it, and how that person then engages life is related to the intentional objects forming the aboutness of his or her figures (the lifespace approach). Over time, the contact the organism has forms, patterns, repetitions, and habits. These are the patterns of contact that develop, particularly when the environment is not meeting the needs and the organism must creatively adjust.

This strategy of following the organization of the field can be carried out by a gestalt therapist using a phenomenological attunement to the organising patterns of the client; thus, here is another point at which the unity of gestalt practice may be noted. This supports gestalt therapists to find ways in which life and situations make sense for people, including how they do what they do from some sense of need which may be contemporaneous with patterns of previous attempts at creatively adjusting.

There is also a stance of trusting in the wider organizing abilities (or wisdom) of an organism as opposed to the tendency to focus on the personality traits or parts of an individual (such as cognitions). As Parlett (1991) states – "As Gestalt therapists we know that much of what may appear random or inconsequential is in fact organised; that is, it is meaningful in some context of which we may be partially or completely unaware."

Principle Four: Surrender to the Paradoxical Agency

In gestalt therapy, as opposed to other schools, we do not try to control the individual; that is, we do not *intervene* with the client in order to cause some pre-determined effect. The field theory approach is to be aware of the operation of the contact boundary in the organism-environment field, rather than satisfying the need for the therapist to exercise control of the therapeutic situation.

This is a paradoxical process of searching for balance between choice and acceptance on behalf of both the therapist and the client (as stated before, it relates to the "middle mode"). This paradoxical agency of the therapist is an ability to sense being "in control" by being out of control. It's a matter of letting things happen rather than making things happen.

Examples of such paradoxical agency are found in the arts, music and sports. For example a canoeist is able to go down a rapid and use the surrendering of control to the river to "go with" the flow of the river and actually go back up the rapid. In the same way, a skier in turning will initially speed up and "lose" control in order to regain the control through the Stem Christie maneuver. And a surfer of the waves knows where to stand on the board and how to lean in order to be in the flow of the waves, gravity, the wind and the ocean.

These are all simple metaphors for the "control" or agency of the therapist in field theory, wherein the therapist's surrendering to the field of attempts to control the person or situation leads paradoxically to an agency within the field that brings about change. Latner (2008) refers to this as "destiny" while dialogical therapists describe this as "the between" and this affects the therapy in many ways outside the direct agency of the therapist alone.

Principle Five: Attend to Part-to-Whole Relationship
This strategy seems identical to the first one in this section; indeed, each principle, like a hologram, contains the whole and each part in some way. What this principle enunciates is the importance of the elements of the whole as well as the whole itself, and the awareness, dialogue, and movement between each for the therapist. The focus is therefore on *the relationship between* the whole and the elements.

This relationship of the one-to-the-whole and the whole-to-the-one is a core principle of the field perspective in gestalt therapy. The whole that exists in the field, such as a dyad or a group of people in systemized contact, influences the behavior and the nature of the individual, described by Lewin's equation $B = f (P, E)$ as a person's state corresponding to the behavior in the situation (Lewin 1952). There are times when the therapist will attend to the importance of the singularity and uniqueness of the person, while at other times noting the importance of the relationship within the therapist-client dyad. This movement between the individual and the therapist-client dyad is often done with some degree of choice on behalf of either the therapist or client and is directed by the organismic needs of each and the primacy required by the relationship. There are times, therefore, when the needs of the individual outweigh the needs of the dyad and other times when the dyad's needs outweigh those of the individual.

Principle Six: Watch for the Field in Action
Develop sensitivity to the field – to the way harmony emerges from chaos. The field perspective supports gestalt therapists to

take the step of being aware of the "self" of the field. Such a perspective allows for the awareness of patterns of the larger whole at work, patterns of homeostasis, polarisation and growth. As previously mentioned these have been explicated in terms of contact boundary dynamics (Gaffney 2006), the life space of Lewin, the cycle of experience (Woldt and Toman 2005), the contact sequence (Perls, Hefferline, and Goodman, 1951) and the contact episode (Polster and Polster 1973). In essence these are all maps to uncover the harmonics underlying the apparent chaos of these aggregates.

Further, there is in the ground of an organism-environment field, whether individual, couple, group or community, an existing implicate order which is available to become figural and unfolded (Bohm & Hiley 1993, Francis 2005, O'Neill 2008). Gestalt therapists are interested in both the explicate and implicate orders of the field. In many ways, then, the work of the therapist is to be aware of, connect with, and experiment with the field.

Principle Seven: Being Present to Emergent Creation
Creativity has been given attention in gestalt therapy (Zinker 1994); yet, as with other concepts, the definition of creativity has not always been consistent with a field perspective and has, at times, resembled more of a synthesis with other disciplines and practices. This has resulted in the notion of the "co-creation" of the field, or of reality, by the individuals who are part of it, i.e., a dyad or a group.

Creativity, however, is an emergent feature of the field as opposed to an amalgam of its parts. Creation does not come from each individual, nor the sum, or co-creation of individuals together. It is an emergent property of the field in motion; it

161

depends on the way the field works, including all its parts, but creativity is the generative nature of the field, and each creative act results in the expansion of the field to some degree.

We would like to propose that emergent creation is the creative action of the greater whole and as such is different, and more, than the sum of the creations of each part. A good example of this was seen in the case study in the appearance of the figure of the gloves.

The most parsimonious explanation for this figure of the gloves requires a field to be in existence that consists of both therapist and client connected through the operation of this field, in essence a "wireless" connection, and not one which is through the interplay of separate contacts and figure formations. This was a creation that emerged from the field and supervened upon the agency of its individual members.

A more co-created figure was that of the three lovers becoming one, in that the therapist could be said to have been "affected" by the figure formation of the client as she spoke about her lovers. Hence the figure was languaged by the therapist to describe their experience of the client.

Similarly the sharing of the impact of the client's glances on the therapist belonged to both the client (glances) and the therapist (reaction to glances) and can be explained by connections which are explicit and shared and this can be languaged as "co-creation".

However the sharing of the figure of the glove which became repetitively figural for the therapist and refused to go away, had no explicit connection to the client or their story or the meaning attribution that arose. This was clearly not co-created in the sense that the three lovers and the glances were. This was a figure which emerged from the field of the implicit reality (or implicate order) of the client-therapist field and so to discriminate this from other creations which are more explicitly co-created, we would like to term this *emergent creation* in that it is created and emerges from the implicate order of the field.

Work of the Therapist.

The work of the therapist is to attend to and be aware of the ways in which client and therapist handle these implicit realities, particularly in how they manifest internally in proprioceptive experience and imagery and the figure-ground formation evolving for each of them. As one starts to sense the field, an identity develops for the therapy dyad – *as a self*. One might see, for example, the people reflecting their mutual involvement by saying things like, "*We both* are surprised that a simple image of a glove can mean so much!" This knowingness can lead one to start understanding that there are two "realities" at play – one clearly evident to the perceptual capacities of the two people in question and another more subtle reality which is of the *self* of the therapy dyad. Contemplating this, one starts to understand that although the self-of-the-dyad is not a visible reality, it is, nonetheless, real.

One consequence of adopting this field perspective is that a consistent phenomenological method would require the therapist to observe her own experience in the client-therapist field and to self-disclose that as one aspect of the experience of the self-of-the-dyad; she would do that rather than only noticing what the client does.

The compass needle of proprioceptive experience, imagery and external figure-ground formation can be the guides to the therapist in this more intimate setting of individual field therapy work. The work thus is being able to be aware of, attend to and experiment with these rich figures which present. We saw this with the case study when the three lovers became one, when the therapist shared his awareness of the glances of the client and what this meant, and the shared intimacy of the gloves, which was such a strong figure for the therapist and held significant and transforming immediacy for the client.

We envision four ways of being that are practiced by gestalt therapists and indicate they are operating from a field perspective.

Being Field Sensitive

Being field sensitive requires the development of contextual sensitivity, what some might call a poetic capacity to see and to hear, to feel, to taste, and to smell one's embeddedness. A field sensitive approach in practice is one in which the therapist attends to whatever becomes a figural event though it may not at first seem organized or meaningful. This differs from the phenomenological method in that the therapist is bracketing assumptions and theories about what is or what is not significant in *whatever* comes up between the therapist and client rather than just observing the experience of the client.

The work of the therapist is thus to trust in the process knowing that patterns will emerge. This practice is also learning not to "force" a pattern or meaning, nor to attempt to work these out analytically or cognitively, but to allow meaning to emerge from the field and within a dialogue with a client. Gestalt therapy practice is thus guided by the figure – ground formation of client, therapist and other selves. In the life space we discover meaning; in the way in which the person organizes his or her world the implicit needs and drives become understandable.

The therapist seeks elaboration of the field and the figures which emerge, including the process of choosing one meaning as opposed to another, exploring our proprioceptive and imagery awareness, and identifying awareness that emerges from an individual or dyadic space.

Being Field Insightful

Gestalt therapists comprehend that in therapy they are dealing with a wide field of influence and connection; so, they maintain a fluid openness to possible networks of people, events and situations. Being field insightful means giving relevance to each event as not random but ordered and seeking to make explicit this order by inquiry and experiment. In this way the gestalt therapist is constantly an action researcher, finding out the meaning and connections being made by the client. Being field insightful also means maintaining a relativistic appreciation of the reality of the field; the person will always have a relative view of this from within the field.

Thus gestalt therapists will accept that while they may feel their view is the right one, there is space for the other view as part of comprehending a wider reality. This does not mean giving up one's view but realizing there are more or different views being held by others. As Parlett states, there is a willingness to address and investigate theorganised, interconnected, interdependent, interactive nature of complex human phenomena. (Parlett, 2005)

Being Field Affecting

Being field affecting means the therapist being purposeful toward and mindful of how changing elements in the field have an impact. The practice of this process is observed in the inquiry of gestalt therapists regarding how the contacts the person experiences in the present moment are self defining and changing as the context changes. Being field affecting dovetails with experimental freedom; it supports experimentation and inquiry around such things as asking, "What would happen if the context were to change; in what ways might self change?" Being field affecting is also manifest in the exploring of situations through process questions such as "what" and "how" and about dimensions of process such as doing, feeling, wanting, imaging, or avoiding. The therapist may seek dialogue with aspects or themes of the work that arise, such as when in the case study he inquired about the lovers being similar and as one, or when the imagery of the gloves was shared. This can also be guided by the principles of the exaggeration/reversal and repetition/reformulation of what figures emerge (as well as the exploration of apparent polarities).

Being Field Present

Ultimately, a field perspective that is enfolded in the practice of dialogical psychotherapy becomes a practice within the field perspective. As well as the traditional aspects of presence, inclusion, commitment to dialogue that the gestalt therapist is guided by when working dialogically, there is the additional field perspective practice of inquiring and exploring the "us" of the therapist-client dyad.

In the field perspective the therapist and client may dialogically explore the experiences where one plus one equals three and the whole is more than the sum of the parts, as in the experience with the glove. The practice of attending to the greater whole that exists and that manifests in therapy is a subtle yet key practice that defines the field perspective in practice and adds a dimension to the gestalt approach.

Conclusion

This presentation of the field perspective in gestalt therapy provides a significant conceptual space to begin research. Noting that there are subtle differences, and not so subtle differences, between the field perspective of gestalt therapy and the contextual concepts of other approaches assists the work of the researcher to begin to delineate and test hypotheses of various sorts. Is there, for instance, any construct validity associated with this term suggested here: "field perspective?" (or for that matter, with the construct of the "self-of-the-dyad?") Are there consilient associations to be made between the field perspective in gestalt therapy and the concept of the "collective" in sociology, the force field of physics, the system in group dynamics and family therapy; is there sufficient discriminant validity among the terms "life space," "organism-environment field," and "field perspective" to assert that they are distinct constructs?

While there is much in common between gestalt therapy and other similar approaches such as systems theory, Lewinian group approaches, and dialogical therapy, there are also subtle differences that we have worked to outline in this chapter. What are the effects of emphasizing the field perspective as opposed to a systems approach? How satisfied are the clients, and, thus, how effective is gestalt therapy when viewed as significantly field theoretical?

It is important that in such a creative modality as gestalt therapy that stylistic difference be supported and upheld. In essence, this is the basis of the famous quote by Laura Perls that for every gestalt therapist there is a gestalt therapy (Perls, L 1992). At the same time, for the ethics of our practice, in training, and in research, we require that the fundamental principles that guide our practice be enunciated. In this way our work as gestalt therapists, however different in style, is informed by a clear theory of practice.

Being Present to the Emergent Creation of the Field: Wordsworth, Buber and Gestalt Therapy.

Abstract

The field perspective in gestalt therapy remains a rich source of controversy and challenge in outlining and articulating a theory of practice. In teaching gestalt therapy, particularly the field perspective, it is useful to find examples of the principles which direct and support practice, as well as enhance and expand theory. Latner offers the field as an inspiring, evocative idea and suggests that when a term such as this has a connotative richness, we can best define it by searching for examples that "speak to us" (Latner, 2008). He offers how he is inspired by the writing of Dogen, a Zen Buddhist teacher writing a thousand years ago, and how he intuitively understands a field universe through his writing. In a similar fashion, Martin Buber and William Wordsworth speak with a connotative richness of *emergent creation* and *paradoxical agency*, two principles of the field perspective recently described in the literature (O'Neill & Gaffney, 2008). This article is an experiment in reaching out for just such connotative richness – an intuitive understanding of these two principles of field theory, *emergent creation* and *paradoxical agency*, to find an articulation of these principles in ways that speak to gestalt practitioners.

> *While with an eye made quiet by the power*
> *Of harmony, and with deep power of joy,*
> *We see into the life of things."*

(Wordsworth, *Lines Composed a Few Miles Above Tintern Abbey, On Re – visiting the Banks of the Wye During a Tour, June 13, 1798*, p.s 104 – 105)

There are blessed moments in the life of every gestalt therapist where they experience in their work a sense of ease, of fluidity, of being attuned to the moment and the context of existence. At such moments the more directive, goal oriented aspects of the self are "made quiet" and out of the chaos of our work with individuals, couples, families, groups, organizations and even communities, a world of harmony becomes apparent. Such moments are manifest and manifold in the arts. We are no longer playing violin solo but are part of the orchestra and music; as a painter we sense that the painting is painting us; and we are so well rehearsed in the play that something more than the words come through and we surf the wave of this new creation. Such experiences are frequently joyful, and bring an expanded sense of self and other, so that "we see into the life of things".

As all students of gestalt therapy would know, the journey to these blessed states of being take many years and it is with furtive longing that we view the work of experienced practitioners and trainers, and with painful, at times shameful, exasperation that we struggle to emulate the apparent effortless wisdom of these masters. As all trainers and supervisors know, such apparent skill only comes through years of ardent work and of learning from our mistakes, and it is with an eventual humble surrender to principles of life greater than those our ego would prefer, that allows us to reap the rewards of practice, practice, practice.

The work of a trainer, supervisor or mentor, while guided by similar principles to that of the practitioner, is also importantly different. While both the pratice and teaching of gestalt rests in gestalt therapy as a philosophy of being, the way in which these principles are lived in teaching is important to distinguish from practice. For example, Tiger Woods may be a great golfer but he goes to a golf coach to help him improve his game, as there are different skills and attitudes required in the "preparing for doing" compared to the "doing". Each of course is a form of "doing" yet the work of preparation, of training, supervising and mentoring is a learning process which may impart knowledge and even understanding, but cannot, as again trainers and supervisors know, impart the "lived wisdom" where a practitioner allows the efforts of their ego to "go quiet" and surrender to the "power of Harmony" and thus "see into the life of things".

As described elsewhere (Levine Bar-Yoseph et al, 2008) the training of gestalt therapists has received little attention in the literature. In part this may be due to the challenge in imparting more than the basic skills of counseling and psychotherapy (to which less holistic approaches are amenable) and that the gestalt approach requires a more complex articulation of that which is a "lived wisdom.

Added to this challenge is the complexity of the initial text itself (Perls et al, 1951) and the controversy of the field perspective in gestalt therapy, which has been described as difficult and demanding (Yontef, 1993) and which has tended to divide into two camps of those who prefer the work of Lewin and those who eschew this for the foundational "organism/environment field" of Perls et al. This initial conceptualization of the organism/environment field of Perls, Hefferleine and Goodman (1951) is complex in its simplicity. It presents as an amalgam of esoteric writing, social critique, psychoanalytical terminology and practical exercises on awareness and contact. Since it was written there have been notable developments in gestalt therapy literature to refine or better describe field theory and link theory to practice (Latner, 1983; Yontef, 1993; Parlett, 1993, 1997, 2005; Staemmler, 2006; O'Neill, 2008).

More recently O'Neill and Gaffney (2008) present an integrative articulation of these two field theories in gestalt therapy and apply this conceptualization to therapy with a case study, describing the philosophy and principles of field theory in practice. In this previous work, rather than describing this as field *theory*, this is denoted as a field *perspective* and there is presented a heuristic list of principles which guide practice (common to all field theory approaches) and suitable for application in gestalt therapy research. They have termed this integrative view of field theory as the field perspective to denote it is wider than a single theory alone and that it includes the main elements and commonalities of these theories as applicable to our practice as therapists, as well as trainers.

The One Field in Practice

It is the intention of this current article to thus further explore two of these principles of a field perspective, both from an integrative view of field theory and more importantly to explore a creative way to support training and practice of gestalt therapy. Hence, rather than being a further critique of field theory, the purpose will be simply to extend and expand upon this field perspective by attending in more detail to two of these principles.

The two principles which will be addressed are precisely those which attend to the struggle of trainees and trainers alike, as mentioned above, which require a degree of surrender of the ego to a wider process in the field while at the same time paradoxically and intentionally making use of this expanded awareness as a therapist. These two principles have been described as *Paradoxical Agency* and *Emergent Creation*. It is also the intention of this article to explore these field perspective principles by utilizing other creative sources and writings which "speak to" these principles and which more poetically articulate that which traditional theory cannot help but leave a little dry. The examples which most speak to the author are those of Wordsworth and Buber.

As a reader please note the shift as we move from theoretical articulation to the poetry and back, and how each informs you in its own way. I would suggest for its fuller impact, and to allow the poetry to be appreciated in its own form, that you might consider reading aloud with a pace which allows the grace of the work to speak to you. Hopefully this will support moving between the theory and the poetry, as one might in actual therapy when we find ourselves moving between being present in the moment and at times reflecting and thinking about the process. This thus also demonstrates an alternative teaching method, of using literature or music or art to "inspire" us and remind us of those experiences which do not dwell in the heady world of theory alone and which hopefully enhance and delight our theoretical musing and direct our choice as we practice theoretical principles, to the stage where practice becomes lived authentic being.

This approach of using wider sources than the traditional theory of therapy is discussed by Latner (2008) who described the field as an inspiring, evocative idea which is best thought of as an attitude. He critiques attempts to describe the field as a theory, a rigorous set of interlocking ideas, and prefers to define it as an "evocative field perspective" from which he derives a "constellation of ideas that come out of field thinking"

(Latner, 2008, p. 27). Both Latner and O'Neill & Gaffney coalesce in their writing on the importance of creativity in describing the field in gestalt therapy. As Latner states –

"The field is an encompassing pregnancy, a potentiality that becomes actual and takes a specific form from contact. Its nature is spontaneous and ephemeral; its form is fluid, continuously created and recreated." (Latner, 2008, p. 24)

Emergent Creation

O'Neill and Gaffney note that while creativity has been given attention in Gestalt therapy it has not been well defined from a field perspective. They describe creativity from a field perspective as "emergent creation", a figure/ground formation in the field as a whole, in comparison to an experience of creation from an individualistic paradigm, (which includes the co-creation of both individuals together). They propose that emergent creation is a process whereby a figure emerges from the greater whole and, as such, is different and more than the sum of the creations of each part. This is a creation from the field without individual agency or intention – a holistic paradigm of creation as compared to an individualistic one.

In essence, this equates to the agency of the whole towards the parts as aptly defined by Wertheimer when describing the field perspective in Gestalt psychology, when he states –

"There are wholes, the behavior of which is not determined by that of their individual elements, but where the part – processes are themselves determined by the intrinsic nature of the whole" (Wertheimer, 1925 in Ellis 1938, p. 2)

174

This principle wherein a whole determines the behavior of the individual parts is more usual than it might at first seem. It is particularly prevalent in everyday life, where individuals are part of a team and they become swept into the synergy of the functioning of the team – such as with a sporting team, an orchestra or band, a choir, a emergency team in a hospital, a family and community. Even with individual pursuits in arts, theatre, sports, and drama, the combined experience of the performer and the audience can come together to create an experience (or figure) which emerges creatively from the whole and is not dependant on the performer. In therapy the authors describe this creative process as a figure which emerged from the field of the implicit reality (or implicate order) of the client/therapist field (O'Neill & Gaffney, 2008) and so in order to discriminate this from other creations which are more explicitly individually co-created, they chose the term emergent creation in that it is created and emerges from the implicate order of the field.

In the previous work Gaffney describes working with a client involved with three men. He notices that when he mentions one she has a pattern of mentioning the others as well. He notes this as a figural pattern in *her* field or life space. He later notices how she looks at him at times and this reminds him of his father when he was angry. Eventually he risks sharing this and she tells him this does not apply to her. This figure has emerged from *his* field or life space. Later in another session he keeps getting images of gloves and sees no pattern of sense to this in either his or her field. As the image is repetitive he trusts this might have meaning and shares it with her, tentatively. She becomes emotional and relates how when she was young her parents bought her woolen gloves which itched and no matter how often she would lose them they were replaced. She had no choice. Now she was an adult she could afford as many pairs of gloves as she wanted and had a rich collection at home to choose from. This connects with her current difficulty in choice of the men. The figure though has somehow emerged from the wider field of the therapist client dyad and as such is more than just the field or life space of one or the other. It is a figure which connects both in some way and arises beyond the simple individualistic logic of the separate egos and life spaces. As we stated previously, the process whereby an event of the client's past emerged as an image in the therapist and returned to the client is the magic and the mystery of a field approach. While there is no doubt that the process of the gloves image can be, or soon will be, open to a generally acceptable "scientific" explanation, our interest is not in such an explanation as we are more concerned with the experience of this process and its value in a therapeutic setting.

Surrendering to Paradoxical Agency

Such notions of reality as emergent creation are challenging to students and practitioners of gestalt therapy. To accept and work as a therapist from this principle of emergent creation requires a degree of surrender on the part of the student or therapist. O'Neill and Gaffney title this "surrender to paradoxical agency" and describe how in Gestalt therapy, as opposed to other schools, we do not try to measure or "control" the individual as a separate phenomenon.

The field perspective consists of being aware and attuned to the operation of the contact boundary in the organism/environment field, rather than satisfying the need for the therapist to exercise control of the therapeutic situation as in some approaches. That is easier said than done of course, particularly for a student or beginning therapist who is doing their best to apply the theory to practice, and therefore "trying" to exert some form of control over what is happening.

In part, the challenge of allowing and working with emergent creation is a paradoxical process of searching for balance between wilful choice and acceptance of what "is" for both the therapist and client. This is described in the original text of Perls et al (1951) as the middle mode – the space between active and passive functioning, where the person is accepting, attending and growing into the solution, with the substitution of readiness (or faith) for the security of apparent control (Perls, Hefferline and Goodman, 1951).

The original text of Perls et al (1951) asks therapists, from a field perspective, to have faith in something more than their individual agency, to let go of their need for security and control and instead to be present in the moment – to be present to the emergent creation of the field.

This *readiness* of middle mode described by Perls et al (1951) offers a paradoxical agency to the therapist – an ability to sense and chose being "in control" by relinquishing control. They equate this state to one which is more familiar to children and artists, and indeed examples of such paradoxical agency are found aplenty in the arts, music and poetry, such as in the work of William Wordsworth. It is also a state frequently referred to by people who describe spiritual experiences, such a Martin Buber. In teaching gestalt therapy, particularly the field perspective, it is useful to find examples of the principles which direct and support practice, as well as enhance and expand theory. Latner describes the connotative richness of examples that "speak to us" (Latner, 2008). He gives the example of how he is inspired by the writing of Dogen, a Zen Buddhist teacher writing a thousand years ago, an how he intuitively "understands how to think about a field-universe in which each being construes his/her reality as universal" (Latner, 2008, p. 25). In a similar fashion, Martin Buber and William Wordsworth speak with a *connotative richness* about creative emergence and paradoxical agency. So it is in reaching out for an intuitive understanding and enrichment of emergent creation and paradoxical agency that we now turn to Wordsworth and Buber for articulation of these principles of a field perspective. Wordsworth's poetry is popular with many, and in particular he speaks to those who have loosened the bonds of what Charles Tart refers to as Ordinary Waking Consciousness (Tart, 1975), allowing perception and awareness to expand beyond normal everyday affairs. Wordsworth describes a state of awareness neither totally directive nor passive –

> *"That blessed mood,*
> *In which the burden of the mystery,*
> *In which the heavy and the weary weight*
> *Of all this unintelligible world,*
> *Is lightened: – that serene and blessed mood,*
> *In which the affection gently lead us on –*
> *Until the breath of this corporeal frame*
> *And even the motion of our human blood*
> *Almost suspended, we are laid asleep*
> *In body and become a living soul;*
> *While with an eye made quiet by the power*
> *Of harmony, and with deep power of joy,*
> *We see into the life of things."*

(Wordsworth, 1798, (1950), p.s 104 – 105)

Some may at first draw back and wonder at the relevance of this esoteric and mystical language in relation to the practice of gestalt therapy, yet consider the struggles of Goodman in Perls et al (1951) in finding ways to describe similar states of being such as middle mode. This is particularly so when describing the Id state, which reads in a similar fashion, in part, to that described by Wordsworth. Perls et al (1951) used poetic language similar to Wordsworth at times, several times mentioning the "soul" and discuss the nature of poetry and its importance as a language for reality.

Martin Buber, in a similar fashion, is not shy to leap into script which might leave the uninitiated reader behind –

> *"The fiery stuff of all my ability to will seethes tremendously, all that I might do circles around me, still without actuality in the world, flung together and seemingly inseparable, alluring glimpses of powers flicker from all the uttermost bonds; the universe is my temptation, and I achieve being in an instant, with both hands plunged deep into the fire, where the single deed is hidden, the deed which aims at me – now is the moment!"*

(Buber, 1958, p. 51 – 52)

With these words Buber describes the shift from a reign of causality in the world of It, where every event and experience is either caused or causing, to the world of relation, where the I and Thou "freely confront one another in mutual effect, that is neither connected with, nor colored by, causality."

He defines the nature and stance of the paradoxical agency of the therapist poetically, when he avows that destiny and freedom are "promised to each other." By this he means there is a choiceful acceptance of "what is" rather than pursuing control of the situation, as promised by the perspective of causality. He describes this poetically and paradoxically as the "deed which aims at me". He goes on to describe how such a state is only available to those who have the freedom given by knowing relationship and the presence of Thou.

Poetic Practice

It is the task of the trainer and supervisor to envisage ways to create a setting which, though structured, provides the safety and stage wherein the trainee can justifiable let go a little of the need for control and allow themselves to be in the moment. One such exercise developed in training at the Illawarra Gestalt Centre has been borrowed from work with Frank Farrelly and Steve Brigham. It has three steps or stages. Trainees begin by sitting in dyads and we explore first how each person prepares themselves so as to be less distracted and more present. The first experience then involves one person taking the time to be in a state where they feel ready and then at this point they signal the other person to begin talking. As the second person talks the "job" of the first person is to sit silently attuned to the other.

This first part is usually very challenging as students who are being silent and centered want to indicate in all variety of ways that they are, indeed, attending and so some vigorously nod and gesticulate in order to do so. The result, as they discuss afterwards, is that paradoxically such concerns reduce their sense of being present, both for them and the other person. Yet this now offers the student and practitioner a choiceful awareness of being as doing, and not needing to do for the sake of doing.

The next step in the experience is for the silent person to now talk when they want to and to allow this to emerge from whatever takes their own fancy, irrelevant to the person opposite them. Hence as an example the trainer may demonstrate how to talk gobblygook and speak in word salad.

This experience is tremendously freeing for some and alternatively excruciating for others who hold a need to be the "good attentive" therapist and once again, when discussed afterwards, brings fruitful discussions around the balance of overly attending versus relaxing into a spontaneous space.

The final phase of the experience involves the person now being centred and present, as well as sensing their ability to be spontaneous, and using this therapeutically. In this instance the spontaneous responses which are invited are the various images which arise for the therapist. They are thus able to practice being spontaneous therapeutically by sharing whatever images come into their head while the other person talks. They are encouraged to trust in the image and share it (and not further explain it) for the other person. The result is that they experience these images arising spontaneously and outside their ego control, and the person talking begins to make meaning from the images. As with reflective listening, the images may be altered or changed by the person talking and that is also encouraged as a co-created field. One might say "as you talk about your work, I get the sudden image of a cage" and the person may say "well it is but I am aware the door of the cage is open."

This experience also brings both therapist and client outside of the world of "talking about" the issues and more actively accessing a richer language of experience of imagery, similar to that of poetry. In such moments the barrier of talk can dissolve into a mutuality that is evident in the case study above with the image of the gloves and which is described by both Buber and Wordsworth. Wordsworth, like Buber, had a knowing relationship with the presence of Thou, and this appears time and time again in his poetry –

> *"And I have felt*
> *A presence that disturbs me with the joy*
> *Of elevated thoughts; a sense sublime*
> *Of something far more deeply interfused,*
> *Whose dwelling is the light of setting suns,*
> *And the round ocean and the living air,*
> *And the blue sky, and in the mind of man:*
> *A motion and a spirit, that impels*
> *All thinking things, all objects of all thought,*
> *And rolls through all things."*

> *(Wordsworth,W. "Lines composed a few miles above Tintern Abbey"*
> *lines 93 – 103, 1950, p. 106)*

In the Womb we know the Universe, in Birth we forget it.

This state of being they each describe, a state open to emergent creation and accepting paradoxical agency, is seen by both Wordsworth and Buber to be a faculty that already exists and is found by un – learning as much as by new learning. Both are clear that such states of being are available but have been "lost" by a process of psychological "development". Buber presents developmental stages which signify the transition from the life in the womb, which is cosmic in nature, to life in the world of It. The first stage of this development is also a loss, as described in the mystical Jewish saying "in the mother's body man knows

182

the universe, in birth he forgets it", and so is this initial experience of birth a loss as well as a gain.

This change that is happening, unlike the physical birth itself, is not a sudden one but gradual – "time is granted to the child to exchange a spiritual connexion, *relation,* for the natural connection with the world that he gradually loses." (Buber, 1958, p., 25) In a strikingly similar manner to Buber's developmental devolution, Wordsworth describes this evolution and paradoxical devolution of the child into the adult in his poem –

"Our birth is but a sleep and a forgetting;
The Soul that rises with us, our life's Star,
Hath had elsewhere it's setting,
And cometh from afar:
Not in entire forgetfulness,
And not in utter nakedness,
But trailing clouds of glory do we come
From God, who is our home:
Heaven lies about us in our infancy!
Shades of the prison house begin to close
Upon the growing Boy
But he beholds the light, and whence it flows,
He sees it in his joy;
The Youth, who daily further from the east
Must travel, still is Nature's Priest
And by the vision splendid
Is on his way attended;
At length the Man perceives it die away
And fade into the light of common day.

Intimations of Immortality
from Recollections of Early Childhood,
(William Wordsworth, 1950, p.s 542 – 543)

In this poem, similar to Buber, he provides a model of human development which portrays the early years of childhood through to adulthood as one of spiritual devolution or un – development. The child begins "trailing clouds of glory" as with Buber's description of the cosmic nature and awareness in the womb. Wordsworth almost shouts the next developmental stage – "Heaven lies about us in our infancy!" and Buber describes this as the infant's instinct is to make everything into a Thou (Buber, 1958, p. 27).

The stages into adulthood are irrevocably contained in the metaphor of light, or its loss, for the next stage of being a boy is to experience "Shades of the prison house" while still beholding the light and by the stage of being a Youth is still attended by "the vision splendid". It is the man to whom this cosmic inscape dies, as this initial expanded awareness fades "into the light of common day" – the common light of Buber's world of I-It and Causality. Buber is more paradoxical and apposite in his use of light as a metaphor, yet conveys the same meaning when he states "He (the child) has stepped out of the glowing darkness of chaos into the cool light of creation." (Buber, 1958, p. 25)

How sad if that was the end of our developmental process. Yet it is at this point when we reach our mature state as physical and psychological beings that Buber tells how there is a call to return to the initial experiences of the states of awareness and for childhood to re-emerge for the adult. Buber speaks of this developmental process as a movement, like a tidal force, in which the relation of Thou, which the child is born from, gives birth, as it were, to the experience of 'I'. This is a movement, not linear, back and forward, between a sense of relation and a return to the cool light of creation. In this tidal process of back and forth the "I" grows stronger and becomes conscious of "I".

As this happens the discrimination of "not I" also develops, so that "The man who has become conscious of I, that is I-It, stands before things but not over against them in the flow of mutual action" (Buber, 1958, p. 29).

From this stance of I–It the person takes possession of all It and objectifies things with the magnifying glass of observation and the field glasses of remote inspection. In such existential isolation lies the aloneness of the modern world – the person detached from universality and uniqueness. This allows for the co-ordination and causal control of these objects, and the desired security of the illusion of control.

A World that is ordered is not the World Order.

Yet this cool light of creation, this age of Causality, is not the end point. As Buber states in iconoclastic brevity – "a world that is ordered, is not the world order." (Buber, p. 31) The world of relation, the world of Thou, calls out with a note as the individual stands fully present in the world order.

> *"These moments are immortal, and most transitory of all; no content may be secured from them, but their power invades creation and the knowledge of man, beams of their power stream into the ordered world and dissolve it again and again."* (Buber, p. 31)

All are affected by this call, this note, in one way or another. It may be through illness or death, through a gentle change in life, through marriage or child rearing, or in the pursuit of what one loves doing best. Whatever way it happens the note is sounded and the world of I-It begins to dissolve in deference for the experience of the world of relation. This is the emergent

185

creation of the field. Such experiences challenge and deconstruct the world of Causality and the illusion of control, and demand an acceptance of the paradoxical nature of the agency of the field – of which all are a part.

Some, like Wordsworth, hear this note relatively early, are ready and respond. Most struggle and move back and forward between the coordinated world of order and the relational world order of Thou that surrounds us. Some fight the experience and the stronger the note and the stronger the fight, the greater the illness or disorder that results.

Today many people cling to the world order, get lost in the appearance of job success, of financial security or any of the treasures which attach so easily. Others turn the call into a battle with their demons, or the demons of other people, and miss the "clouds of glory" in the battle. Many try to sedate the call with drugs or alcohol or food – feeding the physical self until it weights down the I-Thou with its gravity of biological processes.

These experiences, these struggles, this sense of loss of order, control and Causality are experienced as a dis-order. The rise of the professional mental health worker and counsellor have created a work force which in many cases is a part of the institutions of order and seek to help the individual reduce the experience of dis-order and restore order once more. Like religion in the past, psychotherapy has developed as a social endeavour to assist in finding order for those who are experiencing these struggles of disorder.

Already the potential trap of therapy becomes evident. If it does not have the ability to transcend the institutionalised world of

Causality, therapy itself becomes part of the problem. It is as an alternative to this trap that gestalt therapy and other approaches developed, and it is the field perspective principles such as emergent creation and paradoxical agency which articulate principles to guide this work.

Initially people enter the therapy process due to struggling with the lack of order and to try to gain control again. Many therapies have been developed to support this aim. Yet the nature of gestalt therapy, instead of offering control *per se* over the experienced symptoms, is to heighten awareness, contact and dialogue with the faith that through being present to "what is", change happens. This change is a developmental change, not a cure for an ill, and from Buber's perspective we enter again, more and more, into the world of relation, of I-Thou.

As both therapists and clients learn, or un-learn, to open to and be present to emergent creation with a sense of paradoxical agency, then a change happens in how they view the world and others. Wordsworth and Buber both note the significant impact this has on relationships in the world – not only with people but also with nature, such as trees and daffodils.

Buber talks of how a tree can be looked at – as a picture, perceived as a movement, classified as a species, subdued in actual presence so it is viewed as an expression of a biological law, and even dissipated in number, by counting it as one of many. In all these contacts the tree remains an object. Yet if he becomes "bound up in relationship to it" the tree is no longer an "It" and he becomes seized by the power of its exclusiveness – a mutuality of I-Thou, the tree itself. (Buber, p. 7 – 8)

The tree is no longer only an It to be numbered, classified or viewed (like clients can be also) and is experienced more fully and mutually *in relationship*. This attitude and experience instructs and hopefully inspires us to remember such mutuality in mental health care and therapy. While assessment and diagnosis have an important role to play, they become full as we also maintain and live the relationship with the "other".

Like Buber, this wealth of relationship with nature is abundant in the poetry of Wordsworth. His most famous poem is perhaps that which begins with "I wandered lonely as a cloud" which tells of this I-Thourelationship with a hill of daffodils. He extends this relation with nature and his environment even more so to the city of London.

The poem, "*Composed Upon Westminster Bridge, Sept, 3rd, 1802*", offers a view of the city early in the morning where Wordsworth senses the very life of the city itself, at a time when the air was still clean and the city flowed easily into the surrounding countryside, long before the congestion, smog and pollution of today.

Composed Upon Westminster Bridge, Sept, 3rd, 1802

> "Earth has not anything to show more fair:
> Dull would he be of soul who could pass by
> A sight so touching in its majesty:
> This City doth, like a garment, wear
> The beauty of the morning, silent, bare,
> Ships, towers, domes, theatres, and temple lie
> Open unto the fields, and to the sky;
> All bright and glittering in the smokeless air.
> Never did sun more beautifully steep

In his first splendour, valley, rock or hill;
Ne'er saw I, never felt, a calm so deep!
The river glideth at his own sweet will;
Dear God! The very houses seem asleep;
And all that mighty heart is lying still!"

(Wordsworth, 1950, p. 474)

It is this very relation to our environment, this movement to I-Thou with nature and animals, that has inspired the work of organisations such as Greenpeace and the politics of ecology which seek to avert the impact of a world used from an I-It stance – to more readily embrace a relationship with our environment, with the greater whole of which all are part. Our world today is, perhaps more than any other time, impacted by our ability to control so many processes through technology and science.

This approach to making use of technologies has also carried over into health care and therapy, so that the application of techniques and modalities is valued, at times rightly so. However it is in balance to this technological ability that an appreciation of emergent creation and paradoxical agency stands out as being so necessary and important. Like the poetry of Wordsworth and the writing of Buber, gestalt therapy stands out as a field perspective which accommodates and enlarges to include the wider environment, "A sight so touching in it majesty."

To Conclude

This wider connection with the greater whole is in part the intention of this article – to inspire therapists and trainers to reach for writing and experiences outside of the traditional therapeutic writing – to find poetry and prose which speak to them with beauty and embolden therapists to surrender to the paradoxical agency of the emergent creation of the field. There is nothing as useful as a good theory, and as teachers aspire to encourage a theory of practice, then ethically what happens is training and practice is guided by principles, which in turn based are on coherent theory.

At the same time, there is learning beyond traditional theory which comes from experience and a way of being in the world. This requires a different approach to learning; both are valid and the more intuitive learning is often found in creative pursuits and in poetry, music, drama, and the visual arts. This article attempts to offer a path of learning in the field perspective by reaching out for an intuitive understanding in the work of Wordsworth and Buber, who provide an articulation of these principles of emergent creation and paradoxical agency.

This brief article has been written as an experiment in finding other sources of artistic expression to encourage the reader, as trainer and therapist, to consider the potential for examining their relationship with the greater whole, as described in the theoretical statement of Wertheimer. To find examples of the principles which direct and support training and practice with a connotative richness by searching for examples that "speak to us" and support how we intuitively understand how to live such principles as emergent creation and paradoxical agency. To inspire them to move with Buber's tidal wash between the world of Causality and the world of relation, between a world that is ordered and the World Orde. To experience the risk of occasionally surrendering to the the intrinsic nature of the whole, of which are all a part.

Relativistic Quantum Field Theory – Implications for Gestalt Therapy

It may be an opportune time in the evolution of Gestalt theory to address how Gestalt therapy and physics have developed the terms "field" and "field theory" and the interrelationships between the two approaches. Gestalt therapist Malcolm Parlett among others has noted certain advances in physics that have moved beyond Maxwell's initial formulation of the electromagnetic field. These include the quantum field, the relativitistic quantum field, and most recently Bohm's and the work of others on relativistic quantum fields. These advanced notions of field are beyond the original field theory speculations of Smuts, Lewin, Wertheimer and some Gestalt therapy theorists. The possible implications of this expanded perception of the field in physics for Gestalt therapy are outlined below both theoretically and clinically.

Arjuna:
What are Nature and Self?
What are the field and its Knower,
knowledge and the object of knowledge?
Teach me about them Krishna.

Krisna:
I am the Knower of the field
in everybody Arjuna.
genuine knowledge means knowing
both the field and the Knower
The Bhagavad Gita

191

This paper is offered as a heuristic device to better understand the impact and application of field theory in Gestalt therapy and to refresh and enrich the dialogue between Gestalt therapy and other domains, specifically physics. In particular, to what extent are the terms 'field' and 'field theory' used as an epistemology (i.e. as a method of obtaining and validating knowledge) and as an ontology (i.e. expressing the nature of being),with the understanding that each term is not exclusive of the other.

In the present state of physics there is an acceptance of 'field' as an ontological reality, although many Gestalt therapy writers relate to 'field' epistemologically as a metaphor or method. Parlett (2005) hinted at the exciting implications for Gestalt therapy in re – visiting the science that originated field theory conceptualisation, and, by extension, to consider the current state of relativistic quantum field theory.Physics began with the simple concepts of mass, force, vectors and inertia that described the mechanics of the world and of the universe. This classical Newtonian physics posits that there are separate objects and separate forces that act on these objects. Similarly, psychology began with theories of inner and external forces that acted on or in the individual through drives, unconscious processes, reinforcement, will and motivation.

In physics a new concept appeared – the field. Beginning with electromagnetism and then light, the concept of field proved experimentally successful in describing and predicting reality. The field was seen at first as a way of representing vectors of force in a schematic drawing of forces (such as gravity), and as such purely a representation of reality.

Field as Representation

The first stage of developing a field perspective of reality was to visualise and map the force that was operating in a field as vectors. At this point the field was used simply as a device, or method to assist with conceptualisation. By drawing these lines of force such as gravity, physicists were able to note the direction of the force, but not use it as a way to explain gravity. At this point it seemed fruitless to attempt to make the field *more* than a representation or model. (Einstein and Infield 1938). Thus, the field remained an epistemological tool – a field *theory* or method.

Field as Real

It was the eventual scientific work with electricity, magnetism and then electromagnetism that began to establish the field as a reality. While Newton's laws defined the motion of the earth as affected by the force of a far away sun, Maxwell's theory was about a "here and now" field, as a whole – not two widely separated events. To Einstein and Infield (1938), this new field conceptualisation was the most important discovery in physics since the time of Newton. With the advent of Maxwell's four equations describing the structure of the electromagnetic field, there was born, in Einstein's words, "a new reality".

> *"The electromagnetic field is, for the modern physicist, as real as the chair on which he sits"* (Einstein and Infield, 1938, p.151)

Thus, the field had shifted from being simply an epistemology to an ontology – no longer just the field as theory, but *the field* as real.

Field and Matter as Real – the Relativistic Quantum Field

Einstein and others had hoped that the shift from theory to reality would lead to a unified field theory, with matter conceptualised as points of concentrated energy in the singular field. Having integrated energy and matter, he now looked for matter as a concentrated form of field. As Einstein believed it was impossible to imagine a surface distinctly separating mass and field. This, and the advent of experiments requiring an acceptance of discontinuous quanta of energy and matter, left Einstein with the unacceptable conclusion that he was left with two realities – matter and field.

> *"The theory of relativity stresses the importance of the field concept in physics. But we have not yet succeeded in formulating a pure field physics. For the present we must still assume the existence of both: field and matter."*
>
> *(Einstein and Infield, 1938 p. 245)*

The existence of these two realities, field and matter, as described in relativity theory and quantum physics together, led to the naming of such as Relativistic Quantum Field Theory (Bohm, 1993). Separately neither relativity theory nor quantum theory fully explains the phenomenon of light although together, as relativistic quantum field theory, they do.

Field theory in Psychology and Gestalt therapy

While physics en masse re – invented itself from the frame of Newtonian physics to that of relativistic quantum field theory, the majority of psychology remained in the framework of the reductionist world of Descartes and Newton, wherein separate individuals can be measured, experimented on and predicted.

Some psychologists, like Lewin, adopted an understanding of the field perspective viewing field as a representation or epistemology. Other modern day physicists, saw field as an ontological reality. Gestalt therapy contains both notions of field theory. In the following section we will consider these earlier theorists who described field theory in psychology and their influences on Gestalt therapy's development.

William James

James, often considered the father of American psychology, was one of the earlier psychological pioneers to consider the field as a concept relevant to psychology. He used the term field as a way of understanding the structure of consciousness and sugests that there were "fields of consciousness" rather than the traditional reductionist units of thought, memory, or idea. He states

> *"... it (field of consciousness) is nevertheless there, and helps both to guide our behavior and determine the next movement of our attention. It lies around us like the 'magnetic field', inside of which our centre of energy turns like a compass needle, as the present phase of consciousness alters into its successor."*
>
> *(James 1902 in 1977 edition p. 233)*

James began the speculation that classical Newtonian reality was not sufficient to understand our reality, particularly in psychology.

Gestalt Psychology

Experimental Gestalt psychology and the work of Wertheimer, Koffka, Kohler, Fuchs, Gelb and others had a strong influence on Fritz and Laura Perls. This included the later work of Kurt Goldstein in neurophysiology and Kurt Lewin in social science expanded that influence (Ellis 1938; Bowman 2005). The focus of the Gestalt school was on perception and related areas such as animal experiments, thought, psychical forces, and pathological phenomena (Ellis 1938). In studying the original theory as outlined by Wertheimer, the connection between this and the 1951 work of Perls, Hefferline and Goodman (Perls, Hefferline and Goodman) becomes clear.

The fundamental formula for Gestalt theory, as outlined by Wertheimer (1938) provides a description of the field that is in every way consistent and agreeable with the work of Smuts and Perls, Hefferline and Goodman:

> *"There are wholes, the behavior of which is not determined by that of their individual elements, but where the part – processes are themselves determined by the intrinsic nature of the whole"*
>
> *(Wertheimer, 1925 in Ellis 1938, p. 2)*

Wertheimer saw clearly that Gestalt psychology was not a separate entity in itself, but rather a convergence of scientific and philosophical standpoints. It was equally as functional as mathematics, wherein a formula, whether mathematical or psychological, had a dynamic functional relationship to the whole. This included Gestalt psychology's view of the ego, which was seen as a functional part of the total field, with the whole operating in the field and affecting behavior. The connection to subsequent Gestalt therapy theory is also explicit. The organism is part of a larger field of organism and environment, and the behavioural concepts of stimulus – sensation are replaced by alterations in field conditions and the total reaction of the organism (Wertheimer, 1925). Wertheimer goes further in a statement predating the concept of self in Gestalt therapy by talking of the meaningful, functioning whole of a group of people, such as children or South Sea Islanders. In such situations the "I" rarely stands out alone given that it is the wider organism of the group that exists. Finally, he puts out the challenge that mathematics need not only deal with piecemeal situations but also with the mathematics of the whole. In a predictive fashion he suggests that quantum physics may force mathematicians to consider developing a mathematics of the whole situation.

Kurt Lewin

Lewin (1951) described Field theory as an epistemology (or methodology) in that it is simply a way of understanding reality and not the reality itself. He equates it more to a handicraft, in that methods like field theory can only be understood, learnt and mastered by ongoing practice.

> *"Field theory is probably best characterized as a method; namely, a method of analysing causal relations and building scientific constructs". (Lewin, 1951, p. 45)*

Behind Lewin's field theory is a desire to express human behavior in scientific, mathematical terms. Borrowing from physics, he talks of psychological force, power fields and the direction and velocity of behavior noting the parallel between time – space quanta and his own notion of "time – field – units" (Lewin, 1951, p. 52)

> *"I am convinced that these concepts which we use for the representation of psychological facts, like region, spacial relationship in life force, connectedness and separateness,*

197

belonging, etc., are real spacial concepts in a strict mathematical sense. It is very important for psychology to use these concepts in a strict and consistent way"

(Lewin, 1936, p. 42)

Lewin believed the strict and consistent use of these psychological concepts in mathematics was equivalent to the mathematics of physics. However, he intentionally avoided the use of models from physics since models involve serious dangers. They contain much that is purely arbitrary which goes against the required strict definitions. Hence, it makes sense to Lewin that field theory is a method and not a model.

This aversion to the use of models from physics is perhaps one reason why there is a virtual absence of physics in his work. Lewin makes scant passing reference to electromagnetic and gravitational fields, although he mentions having discussed his work with a leading theoretical physicist.

Lewin notes that physics and philosophy have not done enough analysis of field theory to be helpful to psychology, while psychologists like himself, who have an interest in field theory, have not been successful in making it clear.

"The only excuse I know of is the matter is not very simple".

(Lewin, 1951, p. 43)

It is less the physics of fields and more mathematical modeling that inspired Lewin's field theory as a vehicle (or to use his word, "method"), to hold his quasi – scientific methodology of the mathematics of behavior. The lack of validity for the quantification in numbers of the mathematical terms and formulae he uses is the flaw in his approach. He draws these life spaces and field forces in a similar way in which physicists draw vectors of force. This is clearly not the organism-environment field theory Perls, Hefferline and Goodman, though it may have influenced it. There is no mathematics of behavior, or topological drawings in Perls, Hefferline and Goodman nor any indication that Gestalt therapy is purely scientific epistemology.

Jan Smuts

Smuts (1926) provides significantly more detail than Lewin in outlining the scientific ground used to build his theory. He describes electromagnetic and biological fields and returns his work to connect with relativity and the beginnings of quantum physics. There is no emphasis on the mathematics required to do this. Instead, Smuts uses a language of connection and holism that is strikingly similar to Perls, Hefferline and Goodman.

Smuts pays significant attention to physics, and particularly to the work of Einstein. He believes that while the work of physicists is *"a terror to the uninitiated"* (Smuts, 1926, p. 26), it can be simply and intelligently discussed by distinguishing between the viewpoint and the difficult mathematical processes. This pre-dates the very work Einstein did ten years later in making his theories clearer without mathematical formulae, (Einstein and Infield, 1936).

Smuts places the concept of "field" within the history of science and brings an epistemological cohesiveness and integration to physics, biological and psychological field theory. In doing so Smuts demonstrates an erudite understanding of the field theory of physics and psychological field theory.
In ways more like in Perls, Hefferline and Goodman than in Lewin's description of organism and field, Smuts speaks of "the

system of organic regulation," "co-ordination amongst an indefinitely large number of parts," "self restoration," and the "system of co-operation amongst all its parts which makes them function for the whole". (Smuts, 1926 p. 65). It is by moving beyond mathematics to wholeness as described in Smut's term "holism", that one can appreciate his influence on the theory of field presented in Perls, Hefferline and Goodman – an influence imbedded in physics and biology. Smuts' later work brought physics theory to a level capable of understanding the field of Life and Mind, not only Matter.

In writing akin to the Wave-Particle duality of physics, Smuts writes –

> *"A natural whole has its "field" and the concept of fields will be found most important in this connection also"*
>
> *(Smuts, 1926, p. 96).*

This is strikingly similar to the current view of the wave – particle duality in quantum physics that views matter – field phenomenon as a particle (natural whole) accompanied by its wave function (i.e. field). As Bohm states –

> *"... electrons enter the system one by one. Each one will have its own quantum field..."*
>
> *(Bohm, 1993, p. 410)*

It is in his conceptualisation of Holism that Smuts synthesises the work of quantum theory and what would eventually become Gestalt therapy.

> *"The Field is the source of the grand Ecology of the universe. It is the environment, the Society – vital, friendly,*

educative, creative – of all wholes and all souls. It is not a mere figure of speech or figment of the imagination, but a reality..."

(Smuts, 1926, p. 369)

Field Theory and Gestalt Therapy

There are numerous influences on Gestalt therapy and the theoretical and philosophical ground is indeed rich. Few would disagree that field theory is a core philosophical underpinning. Although the construct of field theory has not been well understood, discussed or applied to practice. In Gestalt therapy there is no clear indication as to whether field theory is predominantly a theory and method of understanding reality (i.e. epistemology) or a description of that which actually exists and is real(i.e. is ontological) or an integration of both.

From the various influences that have shaped its development Gestalt therapy carries both possibilities: field theory is both an epistemological method and an ontological reality. Few gestalt therapists have dared to venture further to relativistic quantum field theory or the holographic field of Bohm (1993) or Sheldrake's (2003) morphogenic fields. It is in the current writings of Parlett(2005) that call for further explorations of field theory.

> *"No discussion of the field in the specialized and relatively small scale arena of Gestalt therapy should ignore the general scientific beliefs of the day.*
>
> *(Parlett 2005 p.61)*

Parlett suggests that it would be ironic if Gestalt therapists were to turn their back on these scientific developments since they might well confirm the emphasis that Gestalt therapy has placed on field theory. The need for such dialogue is the key issue raised herein. Perls, Hefferline and Goodman (1951) offer an ontological description of the field as a whole – an organism-environment field. In essence this is not a field *theory*, simply that there is the field, a conceptualisation similar to Smuts, wherein the field explains the ontological reality of wholes and holism.

Taking Perls, Hefferline and Goodman as the starting point of relevant literature in Gestalt therapy, it is clear that Gestalt therapy could be defined as "field – theoretical" from its outset. While there is no listing of "field theory" in the index or the content page, the book is awash with the conceptualisation of an *"organism/environment"* field, proposed as a reality (ontology) and not only a theory or model (epistemology). It may be fair to argue Perls, Hefferline and Goodman is less field *theoretical* and more field *ontological* – in short, a description of the field as it exists: *"... the original, undistorted, natural approach to life"* (Perls, Hefferline and Goodman, 1984 edition, p. viii).

Yontef (1993) argued that by the 1980's there was no clearly cogent description of field theory and that people espoused being "field theoretical" and talk more about dialogue and phenomenology saying little if anything about field theory itself.

"Frankly I think I am clearer when I discuss phenomenology or Gestalt psychology, even about aspects of field theory, than when I discuss field theory directly. So, out of a good sense of tactics, cowardice, laziness or ignorance, I often teach phenomenology and dialogue and

less often directly discuss field theory".

(Yontef, 1993,p.292)

For instance, Erv Polster, one of gestalt therapy's prominent theorists, give more attention in his writing to awareness, dialogue and experiment and with little direct attention to field theory and its application.

"Though I have long been a Gestalt therapist, I confess I have never been a student of either systems or field theory, nor have I ever written about either of them".

(Polster 1999, p.264)

Polster feels more at home with the generic notion of holism and feels that his views do find resonance with Kurt Lewin. Joel Latner (1983), Malcolm Parlett (1993, 1997), and Yontef have reversed this trend of sparse writing on field theory. Parlett (1993) in particular, presents as an advocate for the work of Kurt Lewin. Later works by authors such as McKewen (1997), Zinker (1994), Wheeler (1991), Resnick (1995), Crocker (1999) and others have brought field theory more into the foreground of our literature. By many accounts field theory is the most challenging area in our conceptualisation, training and practice of Gestalt therapy.

"Talking and reading about field theory and understanding it is very difficult, perhaps the most difficult aspect of Gestalt therapy theory to discuss"

Robine (2001) points out that there also a variety of ways in which people have used the term field theory: the organism/environment field of Perls and Goodman referring to a background or environmental context; the Lewian field of forces; and a phenomenological field. Robine also mentions Sheldrake's morphogenic field in which a field creates form. Francis (2005) lists some current uses of field: the field of experience; the field of the soul; the erotic field; the phenomenological field: and the pre-phenomenological field. He also mentions the work of Sheldrake and Bohm.

The Field – Model, method, metaphor or reality

At times some theoreticians are led to the edge of wondering if this is simply a theory they are describing or something more. Malcolm Parlett draws close to this edge:

> *"One of the confusions that arises for newcomers to field theory relates to what 'the field' actually is. Is it simply a metaphor or analogy, or this there an imputation of some actual 'energy field'. In the author's view the status of the concept is generally metaphorical".*
>
> *(Parlett,1997, p. 19)*

Parlett immediately begins the next sentence with "However..." and goes on to list revolutionary and awesome developments in modern physics and other sciences that indicate a reality to the field. Lewin viewed field theory as method and no more, and Smuts clearly saw this as a way of defining reality. These two influences on Gestalt therapy may be seen in our literature. For instance, Perls, Hefferline and Goodman provide principally an ontological definition of an existing organism/environment, while the work of Yontef (1993) leans more towards the Lewinian notion of an epistimelogical definition. It is, however, Parlett who offers a challenge to the purely epistimelogical nature of field theory in urging us on to consider the implications of recent advances in physics and biology.

Obviously, there are divergent views of field theory in the Gestalt therapy literature, differences that can perhaps be understood in a number of ways. Yontef (1993) in his response to Latner's (1983) work on linking quantum physics to Gestalt therapy, defines three types of field theories in Gestalt therapy: Linear, which is seen to be a mechanistic form of field theory using Newtonian language; Non-linear, which is a more "right brain" universal language field theory, with a spiritual flavour; and the Integrated approach, found in Gestalt psychology that allows for differentiation and wholes conjointly.

Latner, as critiqued by Yontef (1993), used a typology of Newtonian and post Newtonian field theory, and also earlier in the article used a typology of field theory linked to the Gestalt therapy training centres and their various approaches. Yontef was quite critical of this lack of consistency preferring instead a typology based on "conceptualisations and not geography"(p.384).

Relativistic Quantum Field and Gestalt Therapy – A Lived Wisdom

Quantum theory and quantum mechanics have been developed to understand a number of experiments which demonstrate the dual nature of reality. Taking light as a prime example, there are times when light behaves as if it were made up of particles or photons (such as the photoelectric effect), and times when it behaves as a wave phenomenon (such as the bending of light around an object).

More interestingly there are times when light behaves as both a wave and a particle. Sometimes the nature of light as particle or wave is *dependant on whether it is observed or not*. This has become known as the "wave – particle duality" (Einstein and Infield 1938, Bohm 1993, Lightman 2000). The quantum view of reality derived four points that challenge relativity and the classical view of reality: the wave-particle duality just mentioned; the uncertainty of measurement; the nature of the observer in determining reality; and non-locality. These four issues in Quantum physics have important correlations with of the theoretical foundations of Gestalt therapy.

The Wave Particle Duality.

In the famous Double Slit Experiment originated by Thomas Young, a very dim light is passed through two slits in a board onto a screen that produces a pattern, demonstrating light acting as a wave phenomenon. However, when non-interfering glass monitors were attached to the slits, they recorded each photon as they passed through the slits. Hence the photo is acting as a particle, as matter instead of field. When the photon is observed it acts as a particle, yet when not observed, it is a wave phenomenon (Lightman, 2000). A wave- particle duality is one in which identity is both matter and field. This resembles the struggle in Perls, Hefferline and Goodman (1951, 1984 edition) in understanding the "system of contacts" and "agent of growth' duality in the nature of self, although as Crocker (1999) notes, this was not clearly articulated in Perls, Hefferline and Goodman. Hence gestalt theory struggles with a similar duality of relativistic quantum theory. We are a particle (agent of growth) and a wave phenomenon (system of contacts in the organism/environment field). Perls, Hefferline and Goodman's original notion of self correlates with that of physics – we are field and matter, aware of our unique nature and intrinsically part of an organism/environment field – both the field and the

Knower as described by the Bhagavad Gita at the beginning of this article. In Perls, Hefferline and Goodman more attention is paid to the field than to the nature of self. Later formulations of Fritz Perls, evidenced in his Gestalt prayer, focuses on the individualistic, particle nature of self – " You are you, and I am I" (Shepherd, 1976, p.3).

The Phenomenon of Non Locality

The EPR experiment, named after Einstein, Podolsky and Rosen, is the most emphatic description of a quantum experiment in its challenge to both classical physics and to the theory of relativity. This famous experiment presents a connection between two seemingly separate halves of a molecule spinning in opposite directions and at large distances apart. The results of this experiment found that when one half is measured it causes an immediate shift in the other. This result demonstrates "action at a distance" indicative of a wave phenomenon. However this effect occurs at a speed that is instantaneous and therefore seemingly violates the universal constant of light, something later explained by Bohm (1993) as a field phenomenon where active information in the field connects each to the other.

> "It is as if the two particles were in instantaneous two – way communication exchanging active information that enables each particle to 'know' what has happened to the other and to respond accordingly".
>
> (Bohm, 1993, pp 203)

This field connection exemplified by the EPR experiment, is at the heart of Martin Buber's original work *I – Thou*, that provided another lens with which to understand his deeply mystical and personal style of writing. His work has been the ground for the development of dialogical psychotherapy, now a strong influence in Gestalt therapy.

As Buber writes:

> " The human being is not a He or She, bounded from every other He or She, a specific point in space and time within the net of the world; nor is he a nature able to be experienced and described, a loose bundle of named qualities. But with no neighbour and whole in himself, he is Thou and fills the universe."

(Buber,1958, p. 8)

In Gestalt therapy this supports and explains the experience of "I-Thou" in the language of physics as being when a separate individual's awareness shifts to an awareness of its field nature rather than its particle nature, or as Hycner states:

> "By the very recognition that there is something larger present in the therapy situation than just the sum of the total of the individuals physically there, this is already a recognition of the 'more than personal".

(Hycner, p. 97).

In a fashion similar to the two halves of the molecule in the EPR experiment, such awarenesses are separate yet are mysteriously connected. Hycner describes the Hasidism story of the holy sparks, that are 'separated and contained in all things,' yet of the common source of wholeness. To paraphrase this, the meeting as people (containing the holy sparks), is like the two separate molecule halves being nonetheless connected. It is this connection we experience as the "between."

Ontology and the Phenomenological role of the Observer

Bohr (1993) felt that the indivisibility of the wave and particle nature of a quantum of energy meant that the entire phenomenon had to be regarded as a single un-analysable whole. It is this whole that constitutes the entire quantum phenomenon (Bohr, 1961 in Bohm 1993). Thus, in quantum physics we cannot discuss the properties of a particular system apart from the context of the entire experimental arrangement that allows for the observation of such properties that includes both the observer and the measuring apparatus.

The basic and most fundamental aspect of quantum theory is that the whole is more than the sum of the parts. This of course has significant correlation and support for the Gestalt therapy perspective on the human personality. In an attempt to explain the connections between the wholeness of the quantum phenomenon and the separateness of classical Newtonian physics, Van Neuman (Bohm 1993) developed the notion of the "many worlds," a theory that states that before a phenomenon is measured, it has existed in many different potentials, or worlds, and that the very process of measurement, observation or awareness creates one of these worlds. Other physicists found "many worlds" untenable. Instead they describe this process in phenomenological terms as the "many minds" theory. Hence, each of the possible measures of the phenomenon represented a certain perspective of mind, and there are an infinite number of phenomenological quantum level realities that are possible. (Bohm 1993) This supports the Gestalt therapy ontologically – based theory of interpersonal realities that are, on one level co-created, while simultaneously being uniquely individual. In phenomenological terms, our phenomenological field is a 'special case' of the wider existing quantum field potential. Awareness by and of itself has an effect, and as we become aware of each other, we change each other. This supports the current work on relational fields (Yontef, 1993) and allows for the simultaneous co – existence of phenomenological and ontological aspects of the field as described by Crocker (1993).

The Uncertainty of Quantum Control: Individuals and Crowds

As Einstein pointed out, the laws of quantum physics are statistical and therefore cannot measure or control an individual system (Uncertainty Principle) but instead imply a series of repeated measurements. This lead him to believe that:

> *"Quantum physics deals only with aggregations, and its laws are for crowds and not for individuals"*
> *(Einstein and Infield 1938 p286)*

This implied that physicists had to let go of the predictive control of classical Newtonian physics, in deference to the statistical approximations of quantum physics. Likewise in Gestalt therapy, as opposed to other schools, we do not try to measure or "control" the individual as a separate phenomenon. Rather, we study the operation of the contact boundary in the organism/environment field. In line with Bohr, Gestalt therapy works with wholes. Earlier, non field theorists talked about Gestalt therapy and the need for the therapist to exercise control of the therapeutic situation, often defined as "the therapist being able to persuade or coerce the patient into following the procedures he has set" (Fagan and Shepherd, 1970, pp. 91-92).

More current theorists like Hycner (1993) describe this as a paradoxical process of a searching for balance between choice and acceptance. This is perhaps best described in the original text of Perls, Hefferline and Goodman as the "*middle mode*" of being – the space in between active and passive functioning, where the person is accepting, attending and growing into the solution. This is also the substitution of readiness (or faith) for the security of apparent control (Perls, Hefferline and Goodman, 1951; 1984 edition).

Initial clinical and theoretical applications of the relativistic quantum field theory for gestalt therapy

The support given to the holistic and "esoteric" world view of the gestalt therapist, as compared to so many other "research driven" or "scientific" modalities in psychotherapy is the most useful aspect of quantum field theory. While gestalt therapy has not traditionally paid significant attention to the scientific validation of its theories, it is comforting to realise that the principles of Gestalt therapy are supported by the relativistic quantum views of reality. As we have seen, gestalt therapists have been operating and espousing a reality of dialogue, phenomenology and field which are well supported by current world views of physics. In many ways some traditional scientific approaches found in Cognitive Behavior Therapy and other approaches are operating within a classical Newtonian framework that is at best a special and limiting case of the wider reality as described in relativistic quantum field theory. Like quantum physics, Gestalt therapy now calls for a new way of research and new consideration of outcome studies.

Quantum mechanics has shifted from a world where the physicist could justifiably stand outside of that which was being measured, to a world where the measurement and act of measuring determine the nature of that which is being measured. Hence, the observer has become part of the mathematical equation and this has led to a mathematics of awareness in which the awareness of one observer (person or computer), is defined as an equation. This leads to a description of the classical physical world as a special limited case of quantum reality with the notion of any other independent existence, as stated in Perls, Hefferline and Goodman, an illusion. In essence, the quantum world is subtle and the ultimate ground of existence out of which the classical world arises and becomes manifest and *relatively* autonomous through awareness. It is like a figure emerging from the ground in a seemingly permanent way, similar to consciousness.

The important role awareness plays in linking matter and field, manifest and subtle reality, highlights some of the crucial functions of the therapist. Consistent with Gestalt therapy theory, awareness by and of itself has an effect on reality. Our ability to be aware of bridging these two realities, field and matter, means that, in effect, we are, instruments of the field. If indeed quantum and field theory implications are assumed realities, how might we operate as therapists? What follows are some preliminary possibilities offered in a heuristic way as encouragement for further discussion and conceptualisation.

Active Information and Quantum Fields – Group Experience

In the Double Slit Experiment described above, the motion of the particle passing through a slit is determined by information in the quantum field as a whole, as that there exists what is described as "active information" in the quantum field. As the particle reaches certain points in front of the slits, it is "informed" to accelerate or decelerate accordingly, sometimes quite violently (Bohm 1993, p.37). Hence, the information in the quantum field that accompanies a particle that has passed through either slit is available to the other particles as they pass through. This is a field phenomenon that in essence explains non-locality. Furthermore, there is information in the field as a whole that is accessible to individual particles which in turn influences them.

This has rather startling yet observable implications when applied to groups specifically and the gestalt notion of the group as a wider self or "whole", similar to a quantum phenomenon. This can be paraphrased as follows:

If the field (group) has already learnt something, the particle (person) in the field will have its motion determined (make choices) from quantum fields that have already experienced the phenomenon. Such choices are formed from the current field (group) that also includes the field's (group) previous experiences in which the particle (person) was not present.

This information gives us a wider view of the group as a "self" that goes beyond the reality of classical Newtonian in which each person affects the other in the immediate environment in a way that is similar to systems theory. In addition, quantum field theory simultaneously envisions the group as a whole phenomenon that carries active information. Hence changes in the field affect others, even in their absence and later when returning to the group. In this sense we can expect to influence more than our immediate environment when a greater "whole" exists. I have seen Gestalt therapists put these phenomena into action. I recall one example at a conference in which the wider community had split over a dispute. The therapist in one of the small groups began the group by saying that if we are true to our principles we will accept that whatever work we do here will affect the wider field. The group accepted this idea and worked with it, not only for themselves but for the community as a whole. This effect was particularly appropriate since it was an Experiment in Community building.

Sheldrake's (2003) work on morphogenic biological fields adds further support to the notion of action at a distance (non-locality) and the whole phenomenon affected by the field including those parts that are distant. Hence, such new scientific theories inform our understanding that if the group has already learnt something, the person in the field will make choices from fields that have already experienced the phenomenon (e.g. from the current group field which includes its previous experiences in which the person was not present). This is a structuring of the ground, not only passively but actively as a process that both provides information and directs action. As therapists we can initially tune ourselves into being aware of such active and passive processes of information in the field (patterns). We can then feedback these patterns to the group, couple, family or individual, finally offering experiments involving such patterns. Knowing that active and passive forms of information exist in the field supports our work as therapists in looking at the wider patterns of the "group as a whole" and notice what happens as the more passive or "implicit" patterns are made active or "explicit." In many ways, the reality of quantum physics supports what we, as Gestalt therapists, already know and in addition adds a supportive space to encourage more learning and dialogue with physics and physicists to discover these deeper connections. The examples given are primarily used to encourage further dialogue and interest building on the work of others like Parlett and Bohm.

The Effect is in the Form of the Field not the Intensity: Couples

One phenomenon of quantum fields that is often overlooked is that an effect generated in a field is determined solely by its form rather than its intensity. This is much different from the classical reality theory wherein the effect, or ability to do the work, is in direct relation to the available force. For example, moving a ship requires a considerable amount of energy. However, in the quantum field theory, a very weak field can produce a full quantum effect since it is attributed solely to the form and not to the intensity of the field. In many ways this is like the effect of a radio signal telling a ship where to go, wherein the radio wave is not directly pushing or pulling the ship that it guides. (Bohm 1993, pp 37) Action of the Quantum Potential depends only on form not magnitude and therefore its effect may be dominant even when the intensity is small.

We can now consider the direct application of this dynamic in couples counselling (although it applies equally well to groups, families and communities).

When a couple attend for counselling there are certain forms or patterns of interaction which can configure the field and direct the action. Probably the most notable of these in Gestalt therapy is what Lee (2004) has termed the Shame Cycle or Shame Driven Contact Styles. The interesting phenomenon I have observed in working with couples is that independent of the intensity of the issue they are dealing with, the form of these blaming or shaming cycles has the same effect. As in physics, it goes against common sense and intuition to believe that a low intensity issue, such as painting a wall or even buying a box of tissues can have such a strong effect on a couple. Once

215

the typical contact style/blaming cycle begins to form, and independent of the issue itself, the couple can precipitate an argument and feel as hurt over a box of tissues as over a deep betrayal of trust.

At the same time, a couple can learn to trust and heal over little issues as much as big issues. From these implications, we, as therapists, can begin to notice the *form* and to watch for changes in the *form* of contact style rather than the *intensity* of the individual issue with which we are dealing. This applies equally to work with families and groups, where the work with one or more persons can affect the wider system or self of which they are a part.

Conclusion

Relativistic quantum field theory presents a view of reality and self closely akin to that of Gestalt therapy, particularly to the seminal text of Perls, Hefferline and Goodman. As Bohm points out, rather than consider the differences between quantum theory and relativity, the clue to convergence may be found in commonality. The key element shared in common is the notion of unbroken wholeness. Clearly echoing the writing of Smuts and Perls, Hefferline and Goodman, Bohm states –

> *"The forces between particles depend on the wave function of the whole system, so that we have what we may call 'indivisible wholeness'... Thus there is a kind of objective wholeness, reminiscent of the organic wholeness of a living being, in which the very nature of each part depends on the whole."*
>
> *(Bohm 1993, p. 177)*

This is strikingly similar to Perls, Hefferline and Goodman –

"The greatest value in the Gestalt approach perhaps lies in the insight that the whole determines the parts.."
(Perls, Hefferline and Goodman, 1951, p. xi)

This encourages us as therapists to move beyond the individual, reductionist nature of current psychology that sees only the separate nature of the therapist and client contact. To move beyond this point is to develop an awareness of the "self" of the therapist/client dyad, the "self" of the couple, of the "self" of the group and of the community. Such a perspective supports us in seeing patterns of these larger wholes at work, patterns of homeostasis, polarisation and growth. We can apply the cycle of awareness or the Contact Episode (Polsters 1973) as a map to the active information processes underlying the apparent chaos of these aggregates.

As we stretch to these larger selves of couples, families and groups we enter the world of quantum physics. Interestingly to Bohm as to Perls, Hefferline and Goodman, it is contact that denotes identity, an identity in which the basic elements are constantly forming and dissolving in succession. Finally, with the challenges proposed by Parlett, Gestalt therapists can bring the needed framework and methodology to provide more than a reductionist "cure" for the ills of both the individual and society. For it is through field theory, as originally formulated in Perls, Hefferline and Goodman, that we are encouraged to realise the impact of a life lived, not only in therapy sessions in a consultation room, but in the way we teach, live and affect the wider field.

There is a trend in certain aspects of Gestalt therapy to engage as private practitioners and as such to be just one more school of therapy. Instead, we can take up and live the challenges of our founders and be agents of growth, change and radical development in society at large.

In the state of the world today, we clearly need more of both, in particular   the   latter.

Drug Courts – A Commentary

Commentary on Joyce Wheeler's Article
Wheeler, J., (2005) Witness for the Client: A Judge's Role in Increasing Awareness in the Defendant. Gestalt Review, *9 (2): 144 – 161*

Brian O'Neill

Abtract
A Drug Court takes place within a wider organism/environment field, and in New South Wales, Australia, Drug Courts have been trialed as part of the unique Drug Summit instigated by the State Government. This article considers the various phenomenological realities from which Drug Courts can be viewed. It offers that in some ways Drug Courts are a creative adjustment by the wider society, with the focus of such problems solely placed unto the illicit drug user. The article proposes possibilities for extension of the phenomenological inquiry and dialogical relationship within Drug Courts to further support the work by Wheeler, and counteract the potential scapegoating of illicit drug users.

> *"And you who would understand justice, how shall you unless you look upon all deeds in the fullness of light"*
> *The Prophet,*
> Kahlil Gibran

It was in the late 1970's in a health region just south of Sydney, Australia, that I began work as a psychologist in Drug and Alcohol Services. These services were meagre at the time and we frequently transported people the one hour drive to Sydney to access services. It was on one such trip that I was driving a client, who was in a detoxification centre, to a court appearance in Sydney. I had also been asked to appear on his behalf by his probation officer.

He was a tall and amicable guy and easy going underneath the exterior toughness he manifested to the world. His stay at the unit had helped him with his drug problem and he was in that phase of recovery where he saw and felt the value of relationships with others that were not the usual "what can I get" type.

He'd been to prison before and was accepting that he may have to go back again. However his new found sense of relationship with himself and others seemed to give some hope that this would be part of a new life.

When we arrived at the courthouse he went into the remand cells and I went into the court room. He came into the dock, the judge entered and the court case began. I was called forward at the appropriate time and spoke of his current involvement in the treatment program and his progress in maintaining a drug free lifestyle, which the judge seemed impressed by. The judge asked me questions about the treatment centre and gained an overall perspective of the program.

The time came for sentencing and the man I had driven up in the car was found guilty and sentenced to six months in jail. The police took him away and I never saw him again.

On the empty drive home the seat beside me spoke with his presence, and I was struck by the experience that courts had such power over people's lives. I was mystified as to the decision by the judge to jail this man when he clearly was making attempts to change his life.

Twenty years later I returned to work in the Drug and Alcohol field after a long stint as a clinician and then academic in Mental Health Services and psychiatry. This time I was the regional director of Drug, Alcohol and HIV/AIDS services and was seconded to head office in Sydney to be the Acting Director of the State Drug Treatment Unit at the time of the Drug Summit. The New South Wales Drug Summit was a most unusual event wherein the State Government sat for an entire week in parliament with a host of experts and clinicians to determine new state policy and strategy for treatment of drug abuse. Most of this was televised and highly emotional at times as many politicians also had close friends and relatives who had suffered from drug abuse.

My role involved the oversight of the treatment and intervention aspects of the State Drug Summit, to progress the new Drug Treatment Plan and to deal with the Federal Government in their funding of the Drug Diversion Initiatives which included the Drug Courts. I was now working on such issues across quite a layered or even laminated field (Parlett, 1993) as displayed below –

- Federal Government
- State Government
- Health Region
- Local Councils
- Drug Courts
- Drug Diversion Teams
- Individuals

In naming each of these aspects of the field as "Health Region" or "Drug Court" there is a convenient illusion of a separate identity and reality, not unlike the original description given by Perls, Hefferleine and Goodman (1951) wherein the organism such as an animal is plausibly spoken of "as if" it is a separate self when in actuality this is always an interacting field we are referring to and not an isolated animal – an organism/environment field. The separate self is an illusion.

If we are willing to take a leap of faith and view these aspects of the field in this way (as interacting levels of an organism/environment field) then a subtle awareness arise. To begin with there are clear boundaries which can be experienced in contacting individuals and the wider systems they are a part of. These boundaries signify a self in operation. Hence just as an individual is a self, so too is a drug court and local council. Thus each of these aspects of the field mentioned above (e.g. a Drug Court or a State Government) are not only a collection of individuals like so many bees, but each is also distinctly a bee hive or a "self".

This bee hive is as much a "self" as the individual, just more complex. As the self gets bigger, such as a State Government, there exists a wider field of bee hives. As we become aware of each of these "selves" in the organism/environment field, they unfold a culture and style of what might be called a personality. So what, we might ask is the personality of a team, a local council body, a Health Department?

For example in dealing with a person from the Federal Government who was funding the NSW Government to provide Drug Courts, I was aware of the political phenomenology guiding his contact with me and at the same time became aware of his individual phenomenology and his understanding of drug problems. Being able to see these various levels of phenomenology becomes second nature to a bureaucrat, even though they may not describe this in such terms. There is a lovely saying in such circles – "the more you climb the ladder, the more you become a servant of the organisation".

As a drug and alcohol clinician I am more attuned through habit now to seek out people's phenomenological understanding of what causes drug problems. There are four main categories of these models as described by Helen Nowlis (Nowlis, 1975). The Moral-Legal models see that some drugs are bad and therefore we need to make laws to stop people using them, and those who are criminal must be punished. These models fall to pieces under scientific, logical, historical and socio-political scrutiny, yet they are the very models most imbedded in people and cultures – they are like a hypothalamic trigger when drugs are mentioned. Such models inform media, are held by voters and hence are taken up in varying degrees by law makers, governments and legal systems. You might say this social and individual phenomenology is a constant background hue in the wider organism/environment field.

It is the very existence of these Moral-Legal models of causation which are the dominant phenomenology of so many of these aspects of the field I have described that have lead to the very need for, and existence of Drug Courts in the first place.

The second type of theory of causation is the Medical Model or the Public Health Model. This approach considers drug and alcohol abuse from a medical and biochemical phenomenology. Drugs are neither good nor bad per se. They have certain effects and cause tolerance and withdrawal. Causation is then defined by drug effects and genetics and treatment is also therefore chemical and biological as well as educational. Hence the wonderful notion of having warnings by the surgeon general on cigarette packets to say "smoking can kill" – while governments collect taxes for this deadliest of drugs and people continue to attend to their addiction. There are no Drug Courts for cigarette smokers. What might happen if pregnant mothers were taken to court for the effects of smoking or of alcohol on the fetus?

The third type of theory of causation is the Psycho-Social model which looks to individual and small group causes of drug and alcohol abuse. Such models have covered a spectrum of theories from the addictive personality, to family dynamics, social modeling, correlations to child abuse and dual diagnosis.

The fourth group of theories of causation is those which are socio-cultural. These models of drug abuse consider that which is in the culture or society which contributes to or effects drug abuse. As with the previous models there are multiple theories and they consider variables such as class, social status, political economy, culture beliefs and sub – cultures. There are some interesting perspectives which consider drug and alcohol industries, both legal and illegal, which benefit from and have reason to maintain the current use level of these chemicals. Hence governments, for example, gain large tax dollars from the sale of such products and even the health welfare and court systems are themselves paid for and supported by people's use of drugs.

A fifth model which I ascribed to early in my career was to see that all these models are applicable in some way. Rather than become lost or confused in the complexity of these competing models, and try to choose which model is most valid, it is possible instead to define a profoundly simple synthesis. In essence each level of causation of drug and alcohol abuse, from a person to a society, is in some way a combination of the interaction of the Drug, the Person and the Environment. Each of these elements has a unique valence for each situation and no one situation, from an individual to a society, is exactly alike in how each of these elements contributes to drug abuse.

The challenge for a clinician, a manager, a judge, a Drug Diversion Team, a Local Council and a State or Federal Government is to discover more about these interacting factors in their own particular setting and to determine to what extent they themselves are, of course, connected to and influenced by these factors.

However before a judge, or clinician, politician or bureaucrat can begin to understand the connectedness that exists between these elements and their own contact with drug and alcohol problems, they face a bigger challenge. All must first have the capability to begin a phenomenological inquiry process which enables them to first see that they themselves hold a model or phenomenological lens which colors their understanding and contact within the field. This is perhaps the hardest part – to be able to learn to bracket our phenomenology when dealing with such powerful emotive issues such as drug abuse.

At each level of the field, from individual to Federal Government, the possible mixtures of these hues of causation make a black and white choice so much more attractive. This is even more so when the true hard drugs, as measured by criteria such as death, withdrawal, social and economical impact, are still those which are legal.

There is the wonderful creative adjustment which takes places wherein the illegal drug user is clearly seen as the "one with the problem" and this affords a sense of security to the rest of the field which can then continue to abuse other legal substances and processes. This projection by the wider field unto the individual and collective culture of the illicit drug user is in many ways supported by the development of drug courts. Yet this is also only part of the picture. The movement to adopt drug courts and what they can achieve and the humanization of the relationships within these fields is clearly a step in the right direction and only a perverse political activist would argue against such initiatives.

By careful phenomenological inquiry across all these levels of the field, we can begin to see that there is not this separate individual alone called a drug addict. As the complexity of this multi-layered interacting field becomes more phenomenologically available and dialogically present, then the ecology of how we treat the "drug addict" will become more apparent. So for example the work of the judge in Joyce Wheeler's article can extend further. She has begun by noting the role of the judge in raising awareness of the person with drug problems, and can also begin to see the extent to which the person with the problem is raising the awareness of the judge. However this is the first step of considering the interconnectedness of such a rich field and becoming more "field sensitive".

The judge and the drug court team may choose to shift roles from witness to decision maker in order to better support the client's recovery and hold the client accountable for their own behaviors, as described by Wheeler. The challenge is next for the judge and the drug court team to encourage the client to be a witness to the process in order to inform *them* (the judge and the drug court team) about their own role in contributing to drug abuse problems.

The client might be also encouraged to inform the judge and drug court team how *they* might be more accountable for their behaviors. This reversal of the previous figure is to demonstrate that the drug court process could extend further by staff being willing to experiment with any fixed gestalts that exist in the field, using both reversal and exaggeration. This experimenting with presumed phenomological "givens" will allow for greater awareness of the field and create a more equal dialogical relationship, albeit proscribed by a court setting.

Hence these theoretical challenges I am offering could be easily carried out by the staff asking themselves and/or the person in the drug court the following sort of phenomenological inquiry questions.

"How do we as a Drug Court contribute to the drug problem, both for this individual and in the wider society?"
"What could we do better to assist recovery?"
"What are we learning about ourselves (judge and team) as we make contact with each person who comes to court?"
"What are we doing, feeling, avoiding, imagining, and wanting?"

These are but a few of the extensions to the process of awareness and dialogical meeting that are possible in this situation. When I worked as a Director of a regional Drug and Alcohol service, I was able to experience these very processes in my own work with both clients and staff. For example when a staff member who was undergoing a disciplinary review blurted out "You just want to get rid of me, don't you... I'm a nuisance to you." I hesitated for a moment.

I knew the personnel officer with me would in no way expect me to admit to this, even if it was true, as it would make the case of the organisation so much weaker. However I took a risk and said "Yes, part of me would like you to move on and not have to be bothered with this AND part of me would prefer we sort this out... just like I imagine part of you would like to work this out while another part would like to just stick it to the organisation. And I believe if I acted from the part of me that wants the easy way out of just having you resign then that would not only be negative for you, it would be negative for me also". The personnel officer was stunned, however the staff member became more relieved and said that this was true, thanked me for my honesty and said that they would prefer to work this out...and they did.

So I wonder what might happen if judges and drug court teams experimented with not only developing more awareness for the person in the court and with also being more dialogically present and considering to what extent are they all co-creating the problems and also co-creating the solutions to drug abuse.

In essence a phenomenlogical and dialogical challenge for the judge and the drug court team is in the following question.

"How is the person in the court room our teacher and judge?"

More and more through the humanization of the roles of judges, lawyers, clients and clinicians, will we see the melting of these frozen gestalten of rigid models of criminality and treatment. We can begin to see that when a judge sends a person to jail for crimes which are principally drug use crimes, then the judge and the court system are not only harming the individual, the judge and the court system are likewise harming themselves. And as the judge and the court system become more human and connected in their contact with the person, then the judge and the court system and the lawyers and bureaucrats can likewise share in the triumph of the human spirit in overcoming this malady.

Hopefully the advent of a Gestalt therapist working as a judge in a Drug Court is the sign of a time to come when the society at large will be willing to let go of the security of "dealing with" the drug abuse problem and instead live with faith in our readiness of accepting, attending and growing together into a solution.

"Often times I have heard you speak of one who commits a wrong as though he were not one of you, but a stranger unto you and an intruder upon your world.
But I say that even as the holy and the righteous cannot rise above beyond the highest which is in each one of you,
So the wicked and the weak cannot fall lower than the lowest which is in you also.
And a single leaf turns not yellow but with the silent knowledge of the whole tree."

The Prophet,
Kahlil Gibran

References and Bibliography

Agazarian, Y.M. & Peters, R. (1981). *The Visible and Invisible Group*. London, England: Tavistock/Routledge.

Alevras, J.S.A & Wepman, B.J. (1980). Application of Gestalt Therapy Principles to Organizational Consultation. *Beyond the Hot Seat- Gestalt*

Aylward, J. (1999). The Contribution of Paul Goodman to the Clinical, Social, and Political Implications of Boundary Disturbance, *Gestalt Review*, vol 3,3 pp 107-119.

Barber P. (2006). Group as Teacher: The Gestalt Informed Peer-Learning Community as a Transpersonal Vehicle for Organisational Healing, *Gestalt Review*, Vol 10, 1, pp 60-83.

Bateson, Gregory (2000). *Steps to an Ecology of Mind,* University of Chicago Press.

Beisser, A.R. (1970). The Paradoxical Theory of Change. *Gestalt Therapy Now,* Edited by Fagen & Shepherd. Science and Behavior Books.

Bertalanffy, V. (1950). An Outline for General Systems Theory" in the *British Journal for the Philosophy of Science*, Vol 1, No. 2.

Blom, S. [in press]. *Organizational identity – A Gestalt Perspective.* Derby, England: University of Derby Ph. D. Thesis.

Bohm, D & Hiley, B.J. (1993). The Undivided Universe. Routledge, London.

Bohr, N. (1961). Atomic Physics and Human Knowledge, Science Editions, New York.

Bowditch, J.L. & Buono, A.F. (2011). A Primer on Organisational Behaviour"6th Edition, Wiley, New Jersey.

Bowman, C. (2005). The History and Development of Gestalt Therapy in Woldt, A. and Toman, S.(2005) Gestalt Therapy: History, Theory, Practice. SAGE Publications, Thousand Oaks.

Buber, M., (1958). I-Thou, Scribner Books, New York

Capra, F. (1982). The Tao of Physics, Flamingo, London.

Clark, N & Fraser, T, (1987). *The Gestalt Approach – An Introduction for Managers and Trainers,* Horsham, UK: Roffey Park.

Crocker, S. (1999). A Well Lived Life: Essays in Gestalt Therapy. GIC Press Cleveland

Einstein, A & Infield, L. (1938). The Evolution of Physics. Simon and Schuster, New York

Ellis, W. ed.,(1938 reprinted 1997). A Source Book of Gestalt Psychology. The Gestalt Journal Press, New York

Fagan, J and Shepherd, I.L. The Tasks of the Therapist in Fagan, J. and Shepherd, I.L. (1970). Gestalt Therapy Now, Science and Behavior Books, Palo Alto.

Francis, T.(2005). Working with the Field. British Gestalt Journal,14,1, pp 26-33.

Friedman, N. (1993). Fritz Perl's 'Layers' and the Empty Chair: A Reconsideration, *The Gestalt Journal*, Vol 16, (2), 94-119

Gaffney, S. (2004). Gestalt at Work – A Case Study. *Gestalt Review*. Vol. 8.3.

Gaffney, S. (2005). On Borders and Boundaries – International Consulting. *The NTL Handbook of Organizational Development and Change.* Brazzel & Jones, Eds. New York, Jossey Bass.

Gaffney, S. [2006]. On Being Absurd – Kierkegaard and Gestalt. *British Gestalt Journal,* Vol. 15/1, pp. 7-15.

Gaffney, S. (2006a). Gestalt with Groups – A Developmental Perspective. *Gestalt Journal of Australia and New Zealand*, 2,(2), 6-28.

Gaffney, S. (2006b). Gestalt with Groups: A Cross Cultural Perspective. *Gestalt Review*, Vol 10, No3 pp 205-218

Gaffney, S. (2008). Gestalt in the North of Ireland: A Blow-in's Perspective, *Gestalt Review*, Vol 12, 1, pp 93-99

Gaffney, S. (2008). Gestalt in Society: the North of Ireland. In Melnick, J. & Nevis, E. [Eds.] *Gestalt and Social Change.* Cape Cod, MA: GISC Press.

Gaffney, S. (2008). Gestalt Group Supervision in a Divided Society. *British Gestalt Journal.* Vol. 17.2,

Gaffney, S. (2008). Respondent in Lead Article. *Studies in Gestalt Therapy.* Vol. 2.1

Gaffney, S. Jensen, I. [in review]. Triple Vision – The Complex Lenses of Gesatlt OSD, *Gestalt Review.*,

Gaffney, S. and O'Neill, B. (2013). The Gestalt Field Perpsective: Methodology and Practice. Ravenwood Press and CreateSpace USA

Gibran, K., (1964). The Prophet, Pan Books, London.

Hycner, R. (1995). The Healing Relationship in Gestalt Therapy: A Dialogic – Self-Psychology Approach.

Inderbitzen, L.B. (1990). The Treatment Alliance. In Levy, S. and Ninan, P. (Eds) *Schizophrenia: Treatment of Acute Psychotic Episodes,* American Psychiatric Press, Washington D.C.

Hamlyn, D.W. (1987). The Penguin History of Western Philosophy. Penguin Books, London.

Herman, S.M & Korenich, M, (1977). *Authentic Management: A Gestalt Orientation to Organizations and Their Development,* Addison-Wesley.

James, W. (1902). The Varieties of Religious Experience, 1977 Fontana Paperback, Glasgow.

Kempler. W., (!974). Principles of Gestalt Family Therapy, Kempler Institute,California.

Kepner, J. (1995). Healing Tasks: Psychotherapy with Adult Survivors of Childhood Abuse. Jossey-Bass and Gestalt Institute of Cleveland, San Francisco.

Kepner, E., and Brien, L, (1971). Gestalt Therapy: A Behavioristic Phenomenology. in Fagan, J & Shepherd, I.L., (eds). *Gestalt Therapy Now*, (pp. 39-46). New York: Harper Colophon.

Latner, J. (1983). This is the speed of light: Field and systems theory in Gestalt therapy. The Gestalt Journal,6,2 (Fall 1983), 71-90

Latner, (2008). Commentary I: relativistic Quantum Field Theory: Implications for Gestalt Therapy, (or The Speed of Light Revisited). Gestalt Review Vol 12, 1, pgs 24-32.

Lee, R. (Ed.). (2004). *The Values of Connection: A Relational Approach to Ethics.* GIC Press, Cleveland

Lee, R.(Ed) (2004). The Values of Connection: A Relational Approach to Ethics. GIC Press, Cleveland.

Le Grand, L.J. (2003). Motivation, agency and Public Policy; Of Knights and Knaves, Pawns and Queens. Oxford, Oxford University Press.

Le Shan, (1974). The Medium, the Mystic and the Physicist. Ballantine Books, New York

Lewin, K. (1936) Principles of Topological Psychology. McGraw-Hill, New York

Lewin, K.(1951). Field Theory in Social Science. University of Chicago Press, Chicago.

Lightman, A (2000). Great Ideas in Physics. McGraw-Hill, New York

Mackewen, J.(1997). Developing Gestalt Counselling, Sage Publications, London.

McNamara, W., (1979). "Mystical Passion - The Art of Christian Loving" San Francisco: Harper & Row, pages 57-58

McTaggart, L. (2003). The Field. Harper Collins, London.

Marrow, A.J, (1969). *The Practical Theorist: The Life and Work of Kurt Lewin,* New York: Basic Books.

Maurer, R. [2005]. Approaches with Organizations and Large Systems. In Woldt, A. & Toman, S.[Eds.] *Gestalt Therapy: History, Theory and Practice.* Thousand Oaks, CA: Sage Publications

Maurer, R. (2008). Connection vs Survival At Work (or Buber meets Machiavelli), *Gestalt Review*, Vol 12,1, pp 43-57

Mitchell, S. (translator) (2000). The Bhagavad Bhagavad Gita. Three Rivers Press, New York.

Nevis, E, (1987), *Organizational Consulting – A Gestalt Approach,* Cleveland, USA: GIC Press.

Nevis, E. (1987, 2005). *Organizational Consulting: A Gestalt Approach.* Cleveland: GestaltPress.

Nicoll, M (1976). Living Time and the Integration of Life. Watkins, London.

Nowlis, H., (1975).Drugs Demystified, The Unesco Press, Paris.

Ornstein, R. (1972). The Psychology of Consciousness, Penguin, New York

O'Neill, B., (2005). Witness for the Client: The Judge's Role in Increasing Awareness in the Defendant, Commentary on Joyce Wheeler's Article, *Gestalt Review*, vol 9,2, pp 162-170.

O'Neill, B., (2008).Post Relativistic Quantum Field Theory and Gestalt Therapy, *Gestalt Review*, Vol 12, no 1, pps 7-23.

O'Neill, B., & O'Neill, J. (2008).*The Use of Group in Training*, in Feder, R., *Beyond the Hot Seat: Group Approaches in Gestalt Therapy*, Gestalt Institute Press, USA.

O'Neill, B., & O'Neill, J. (2008). *Field Theory and Couples Therapy*, in Lee, R., The Secret Language of Intimacy, Routledge Press/Gestalt Press, USA,

O'Neill, B., & Gaffney, S. (2008). *The Application of a Field Perspective Methodology*, in Brownell, P., *Handbook for Theory, Research and Practice in Gestalt Therapy*, Cambridge Scholars Publishing, Cambridge.

O'Neill, B. (2012). *Gestalt Family Therapy* in Levine Bar-Yoseph, T., (ed) New Approaches to Gestalt Therapy, Routledge, London.

Parlett, M.(1993). Towards a More Lewian Gestalt Therapy, British Gestalt Journal,2,2 p. 115-121

Parlett, M.(1997). The Unified Field in Practice. Gestalt Review, 1,1 p.16-33

Parlett, M. (2005). Contemporary Gestalt Therapy: Field Theory in Woldt, A. & Toman, S. Gestalt Therapy: History, Theory and Practice. Sage Publications, Thousand Oaks.

Perls, F., Hefferline, R., & Goodman, P. (1951/1984). *Gestalt Therapy: Excitement and Growth in the Human Personality.* London: Souvenir Press edition.

Perls, F. (1969). *Gestalt therapy verbatim.* The Gestalt J Press Highland, New York.

Perls, F.S. (1971). Four Lectures. in Fagan, J & Shepherd, I.L. (eds) *Gestalt Therapy Now*, (pp.14-38). Harper Colophon, New York.

Petersen, V. C. (2007). Distortions of Modern Management – and an attempt to correct them. CREDO Department of Mangement, Denmark

Philippson. P. (2002). Self in Relation. Gestalt Journal Press, New York.

Plsek, P.E. and Wilson, T. (2010). Complexity, leadership, and management in healthcare organisations British Medical Journal, 29; 323(7315): 746–749.

Polster, E. & Polster, M. (1973). Gestalt therapy integrated: Contours of theory and practice. Brunner-Mazel, New York.

Polster, E., (1993). Individuality and Communality. *The British Gestalt Journal*, Vol 2, 1, pp19-25.

Polster, E & Polster, M. (1999). From the Radical Center: The Heart of Gestalt Therapy. GIC Press, Cleveland.

Resnick, R. (1995). Gestalt therapy: Principles, prisms and perspectives. British Gestalt Journal,4(1),3-13.

Robine, J. (2001). From Field to Situation in Robine, J (Ed) Contact and Relationship in a Field Perspective. L'experimerie Bordeaux.

Rogers, C.R. (1942). *Counselling and Psychotherapy: Newer Concepts in Practice*. Houghton Mifflin, Boston.

Rost, J.C. (1991). Management for the 21st Century, Prager Publications, Westport.

Sheldrake, R.(2003). The Sense of Being Stared At and other aspects of the Extended Mind. Random House, London.

Shepard, M (1976). Fritz. Bantam, New York

Smuts, J. (1926). edited by Holst, S. (1999) Holism and Evolution: The Original Source of the Holistic Approach to Life. Sierra

Sunrise Books.

Staemmler, F.M. (2006). A Babylonian Confusion? – The Term Field. The British Gestalt Journal, 15:2 : 64-83

Starak, Y., Bernet, A., and Maclean, A., (1994). *Grounds for Gestalt*, Christchurch, New Zealand, Foreground Press.

Swedenborg, E. (1768, edition 1992). Conjugial Love, Swedenborg Foundation, New York

Swedenborg, E. (1758, edition 2009). Heaven and Its Wonders and Hell, Swedenborg Foundation, New York pg 31-32

Talbot, M.(1991). The Holographic Universe. Harper Collins, London.

Tart, C., (1975). States of Consciousness. E P Dutton and Co, New York.

The Shorter Oxford Dictionary on Historical Principles, (1973). Oxford University Press, Oxford.

Tiernan, M.J., Morely, S.D., and Foley E.F. (2006). "Modern Management". 3rd Edition, Gill and MacMillan, Dublin.

Van Dusen, W. (1975). Invoking the Actual, in Stevens, J.O., gestalt is, Real People Press, Moab.

Van Dusen, W. (2001). *The Design of Existence*. Chrysalis Books, West Chester,

Weymes, E. (2004). A Challenge to Tradition Management Theory. Foresight, Vol 6, no 6, pgs. 338-348.

Wheeler, G (1991). Gestalt Reconsidered: A New Approach to Contact and Resistance. GIC Press, Cleveland.

Wheeler, G. (2000). *Beyond Individualism: Towards a New Understanding of Self, Relationship and Experience.* Hillsdale, NJ: Gestalt Institute of Cleveland Press.

Wertheimer, M. Gestalt Theory. (1925). in Ellis, W. ed., (1938 reprinted 1997). A Source Book of Gestalt Psychology.The Gestalt Journal Press, New York

Wilber, K. (ed) (1985). The Holographic Paradigm and Other Paradoxes. Shambhala, Boston & London.

Wordsworth, W. in Van Doren, M. (1950). William Wordsworth Selected Poetry, Random House, New York.

Yontef, G. (1993). Awareness, Dialogue and Process: Essays of Gestalt Therapy. The Gestalt Journal Press, New York,

Zinker, J. (1994). In search of good form: Gestalt therapy with couples and families. Jossey- Bass, San Francisco.